Don't Tell Mummy

Toni Maguire

Don't Tell Mummy

A true story of
the ultimate betrayal

HARPER
element

This book is a work of non-fiction based on the recollections of Toni Maguire. Some of the names of people, places, dates and the detail of events have been changed to protect the privacy of others. The author has warranted to the publishers that, except in such minor respects not affecting the substantial accuracy of the work, the contents of this book are true.

HarperElement
An Imprint of HarperCollins*Publishers*
77–85 Fulham Palace Road,
Hammersmith, London W6 8JB

The website address is: www.thorsonselement.com

and *HarperElement* are trademarks of
HarperCollins*Publishers* Ltd

First published by HarperElement 2006
This edition 2007

1 3 5 7 9 10 8 6 4 2

A catalogue record of this book is
available from the British Library

ISBN-13 978-0-00-722376-3
ISBN-10 0-00-722376-5

Printed and bound in Great Britain by
Clays Ltd, St Ives plc

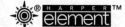

To Caroline

… who opened the door
and encouraged me to walk through

Acknowledgements

Special thanks to Alison, Gerry and Gary, who have so enriched my life.

A big thank you to my agent Barbara Levy for her patience and the best Chinese food.

And thank you, Mavis Cheek, for writing your witty and humorous books, which saw me through the nights at my mother's side.

Don't Tell Mummy

Chapter One

Nothing about the house in the quiet suburb of Belfast made it stand out. The imposing red-brick building stood back from the road surrounded by landscaped gardens. It looked like any other large family home. The number on the gate confirmed I was at the right address as I scanned the piece of paper in my hand for final reassurance.

Not being able to delay any longer, I picked up my suitcase, which the taxi driver had deposited on the pavement, walked down the path and pushed open the door.

'I'm Toni Maguire,' I announced to the casually dressed woman behind the reception desk. 'Ruth Maguire's daughter.'

She looked at me curiously.

'Yes. Your mother told us this morning you were coming. We never knew she had a daughter.'

No, I thought, I don't suppose you did.

'Come, I'll take you to her. She's waiting for you.'

She walked briskly down the corridor to the pretty

four-bedded ward where my mother was. I followed in her wake, hiding my emotions.

Four old ladies reclined in chairs placed in front of their bedside lockers. Three of the lockers were covered in photographs of loved ones whilst the fourth, my mother's, was bare. I felt a familiar stab of pain. Not even one of my baby photos was on display.

She sat in her chair, a blanket over her knees and her legs on the raised footrest. This was not the robust woman who on my last visit to Ireland over a year ago had still looked a decade younger than her birth certificate stated. That woman had been replaced by this shrunken, frail old lady, who looked terminally ill.

The dark green eyes that had so often flashed with anger now welled with tears as she held her arms out to me. Dropping my bags to the floor I went into them. For the first time in many years my mother and I embraced, and my love that had lain dormant resurfaced.

'You've come, Toni,' she murmured.

'I would always have come if you'd asked me,' I replied softly, shocked by the fleshless shoulders I felt through her dressing gown.

A nurse bustled in and tucked the blanket more firmly around my mother's legs. Turning to me she enquired politely about my journey from London.

'Not bad,' I said. 'Only three hours door to door.'

Gratefully, I took a cup of tea from her, staring intently into the cup as I composed myself, not wanting my face to betray the shock that my mother's fragility had given me. She had, I knew, been admitted to the hospice before to monitor her pain control, but I knew this visit would be the last.

Having been informed of my arrival, my mother's doctor came to see me. He was a cheerful, pleasant-looking young man, with a broad smile.

'Ruth,' he asked, 'are you happy now that your daughter has come to see you?'

'Very happy,' she replied in her usual lady-like tones, so expressionless she might have been commenting on the weather.

When he turned to me, I saw the same curious expression that had flitted through the receptionist's eyes.

'May I call you Toni?' he asked. 'It's what your mother called you.'

'Of course.'

'I'd like a couple of words with you when you've finished your tea. Just come down to my room. The nurse will show you where it is.'

After one more reassuring smile to my mother, he left.

Taking a few minutes to postpone what I felt would be a difficult meeting, I sipped my tea slowly before reluctantly going to see what he wanted.

Entering his room I was surprised to find another man sitting beside him, dressed in casual clothes, only his dog collar identifying his calling. I sat down on the only available chair, looked at the doctor with what I hoped was a bland expression and waited for him to start the conversation.

As he gently began to explain the situation my heart sunk. I realized that some answers would be required from me; answers I was reluctant to give, for giving them would mean opening up those memory boxes where the ghost of my childhood lived.

'We have some problems with your mother's treatment and we hoped that maybe you could shed some light on them. The pain-control medication is not working as well as it should. And, to be frank, she's on the maximum dosage we can prescribe.'

He paused to gauge my reaction. Receiving none he continued. 'In the daytime she responds well to the staff, lets them take her to the coffee lounge, shows an interest in her appearance, and she has a good appetite. It's the night-time that's the problem.'

Again he paused and still I kept what I knew was a neutral expression on my face, not yet ready to give anything away. After a few seconds he continued, with slightly less confidence.

'Your mother has very disturbed nights. She wakes extremely distressed and in more pain than she should be. It's almost as though she's fighting against her medication.'

Oh, the witching hours, I thought. I knew those hours so well, where control over thoughts disappears to let the blackest memories surface, jolting us wide awake to feel despair, anger, fear or even guilt. In my case I could get out of bed, make a cup of tea, read or listen to music. But what could my mother do now to allay those dark thoughts?

'Twice she's asked the nurse to call the minister out. But,' he turned to the man beside him, 'my friend tells me that by the time he arrives she's changed her mind about her need to talk to him.'

The minister nodded to confirm this, and I felt the impact of two pairs of eyes searching my face for answers; this time it was the minister who broke the silence, leaning across the desk and putting the next question.

'Toni, is there anything you can tell us to help us help your mother?'

I saw the genuine concern in his face and chose my words carefully.

'I think I understand why my mother's nights might be disturbed. She believes in God. She knows she has a very short time before she meets Him, and I think she is very frightened of dying. I want to help but there is little I can do. I hope for her sake she can find the strength to talk to you.'

The doctor looked puzzled. 'You mean your mother has something on her conscience?'

I thought of just how much my mother had in her past to feel guilty about, wondering if her memories haunted her. I fought not to let my thoughts show, but felt a sigh escape me as I replied.

'She must have. She should have. But whether she'd ever admit she's done anything wrong I don't know. She never has.'

The doctor looked troubled. 'Well, it's certainly affecting the pain control. When the mind is as restless as your mother's seems to be, the medication simply does not work to its full effect.'

'In that case you will just have to monitor it and my mother more closely,' I said, more abruptly than I should as a feeling of helplessness rose in me. With that I returned to my mother's ward.

On entering her eyes held mine.

'What did the doctor want?' she asked.

Knowing that she knew, I looked at her squarely in the face.

'They told me you had called the minister out twice in the middle of the night and that you were very distressed.' Then my courage failed me as it always did. 'But we don't need to worry about it now do we?'

The childhood habit of pandering to her wishes of 'no discussion' remained unbroken.

The rest of that first morning she was very tearful. I knew it was common with terminally ill patients, but it still moved me unbearably. Tenderly, I wiped away her tears, remembering days when as a small child she'd done the same for me. She was more affectionate than she had been for many years: she wanted to hold my hand, she wanted to talk and she wanted to remember happier times. I looked at her now, an old lady whose limited days were unlikely to end as peacefully as I wanted, and realized how badly she needed me.

'How long are you going to stay?' she asked.

'For as long as you need me,' I replied lightly, trying to cover up what I really meant.

My mother, who could always read me, smiled. With a jolt

I was reminded of her much younger self and the times when we'd been so close. I felt the surge of my old love.

'I don't know how long that will be,' she said with a wry smile. 'But I don't think it will be very long.'

She paused, looked at me and asked: 'You've only come, haven't you, because you know I'm dying?'

I squeezed her hand, and rubbed the back of it gently with my thumb. 'I've come because you asked me to. I would always have come if you'd asked. And yes, I have come to help you die in peace, because I believe I'm the one person who can do that.'

I hoped she would find the willpower to talk honestly, and for a short time that first day I believed she would.

Pulling on my hand she said: 'You know, Toni, the days you were a small baby were the happiest times of my life. I remember it as though it was yesterday. When you were born I sat in that hospital bed feeling so proud that at the age of twenty-nine I had produced you. You were such a small, perfect little person. I felt such love for you. I wanted to hold you. I wanted to look after and protect you. I wanted a good life for you. I felt such tenderness and love, that's what I felt then.'

A lump rose in my throat as I remembered many years ago when I had been encircled by her love. Then she was a mother who cuddled and played with me, read stories and tucked me into bed; a mother whose scent I breathed in as she bent down to give me my good-night kiss.

A child's voice infiltrated my memory until the sounds became words whispered in my ear.

'Where did that love disappear to, Toni? Today is your birthday. She says she remembers when you were born. She says how she loved you then, yet fourteen years later she tried to send you to your death. Does she not remember that? Does she not think you do? Has she really blocked it out of her mind? Have you?'

I closed my ears to the voice and willed it to be silent. I wanted to leave my memories in the boxes where they'd been stored for thirty years, never looked at and never thought of except when the witching hours allowed them to escape, when they would hitch a lift on the end of a fading dream. Their ice-cold tentacles would then stroke my subconscious, leaving dim pictures from another time until I awoke to banish them.

Later that day I took her out in her wheelchair around the grounds. She'd always loved creating beautiful gardens; it was as though all her nurturing instincts, which had ceased towards me long ago, went into them.

She asked me to stop at various plants and bushes as she told me their names. Sadly she murmured, more to herself than to me, 'I'll never see my garden again.'

I remembered visiting her at the onset of her illness. I'd gone to Northern Ireland with a friend. Taking advantage of the fact that my father was away for the day, playing golf, I had visited my mother. She had proudly shown me photographs of how her garden had looked before she'd started work, a desolate area with clumps of coarse grass and not even a wild flower to enhance it.

As she walked me around she showed me something that instantly brought a smile to my face. On Mother's Days and birthdays I'd sent her baskets of tiny plants. She showed me how, mixed with others grown from cuttings, she'd replanted them into her eclectic collection of containers, ranging from chimneys and old kitchen sinks to terracotta pots and a drinking trough, creating an explosion of colour around the patio she had designed.

She'd named all the shrubs for me that day too.

'This is my favourite, it's called Buddleia,' she informed me. 'But I like its nickname better, "the butterfly bush".'

As if to give credence to its more popular name a cloud of butterflies hovered over the deep purple shrub, their wings shimmering in the afternoon sunlight. Another area gave off a heady aroma of roses, their petals shading from clotted-cream perfection to a dark rich pink. Another area contained her beloved lilies. In another wild flowers blended with the cultivated ones.

'If they look pretty they're not weeds,' she laughed.

There were pebbled walkways, with arches made of wire, where jasmine and honeysuckle had been lovingly trained to grow and add their perfumes to the air. At the base of one nestled a collection of gnomes.

'My little bit of nonsense,' she called them.

She looked so happy and serene that day that it became a memory I stored in my mental photograph album. One I could take out at will and enjoy.

The next day I drove to a garden centre, bought her a small

summer house to protect her from the elements and had it delivered.

'So that whatever the weather you can always enjoy your garden,' I told her, knowing she wouldn't have more than one more summer to enjoy it.

She had created an English country garden in Northern Ireland, a country she had never taken as her own, always feeling herself a stranger there.

I took that memory out then and felt such sorrow for her, my lonely mother who had created her life out of imagination then turned it into her reality.

There was a side of me that was enjoying being with her in the hospice, despite her frailty. Finally I was able to spend some time alone with her, time I knew was disappearing minute by minute.

That evening I helped put her to bed, brushed her hair back from her brow and kissed her forehead.

'I'll be sleeping in the chair beside your bed,' I told her. 'I'll never be very far away.'

After the nurse had given out sleeping pills, I sat holding her hand, which had grown small and fragile. The skin, streaked with blue veins, seemed almost translucent. Someone had given her a manicure, shaping and polishing the nails into ovals and colouring them a pale pink, unlike the soil-stained ones I remembered from my last visit.

Once she'd fallen asleep I took one of my Mavis Cheek novels and went to the lounge. I felt an overwhelming sorrow that the mother I'd once loved so much was dying; sorrow that for all the harm, for all the things she'd done, she'd never been happy. I grieved for the relationship with her I'd always wanted but which, apart from my very early childhood, I had been denied.

The book remained unread that night as control over my memories deserted me. My mind strayed back to those early days I spent with her, days when I'd felt cherished, protected and loved, days that in my memory were always sunny – until the blackness came.

Antoinette, the child, came to me in that space that twilight creates, when dreams have deserted us but consciousness still slumbers. Dressed in shades of grey, her ivory-white face gleamed up at me from under her ebony fringe.

'Toni,' she whispered, 'why did you never allow me to grow up?'

'Leave me in peace,' I silently cried, summoning all my mental energy to push her away.

My eyes opened and now only dust motes danced in the air, but when I placed my hands on my face they came away damp from a child's tears on adult cheeks.

'Toni,' she whispered, 'let me tell you the story of what really happened. It's time now.'

I knew that Antoinette was awake now and I would not be able to force her to resume the years of slumber that once I had banished her to. Closing my eyes I allowed her whisper to filter into my mind as she started our story.

Chapter Two

My first memories were of my mother and me living in a house with a garden in Kent, where my diminutive grandmother was a frequent and welcome visitor. Upon hearing her voice calling 'Antoinette, where are you?' as she pretended to search for me, I would stop whatever I was doing, rush to greet her and to be hugged in return.

She had a fragrance particular to her, a mixture of face powder and lily of the valley, a scent that in the future always evoked memories of her. I would feel a glow of love between us as I breathed in that aroma.

On sunny days she would suggest leisurely walks towards the main street of Tenterdon, where we would make our way to one of the oak-beamed tearooms. My play clothes would have been exchanged for a clean dress, my face and hands wiped and my hair brushed before I was considered presentable enough for such outings.

Once she had placed high heels on her feet and picked up

a matching handbag, my mother would apply bright red lipstick, fluff powder on her nose and the three of us would set off.

A black-and-white-uniformed waitress would show us to our table, where my grandmother would proceed to order afternoon tea. Scones with jam and cream, followed by individual pink and yellow iced cakes, were washed down by diluted squash for me, tea for the two adults.

My mother, wearing a square-necked dress, her head bare, would chatter companionably to my grandmother, who, always, regardless of the weather, hid her still red-gold hair under a hat. Ladies of a similar age, dressed in printed dresses topped by straw boaters or pillboxes, would greet her with smiles, remark how much I was growing and comment on the weather, a subject which, to my child's ears, grown-ups always showed an inordinate interest in.

Another special outing was when we visited Mrs Trivett, an old school friend of my grandmother's who, to my delight, made homemade sweets in her tiny black and white cottage. Her postage-stamp-sized garden was filled with deep raspberry pink hydrangeas, whose big lacy heads hung over the low brick wall and nodded in the breeze. To my fascination two plump gnomes sat underneath one bush, fishing rods in their hands. Perhaps it was Mrs Trivett who sowed the seeds of my mother's affection for these garden ornaments in later life.

My grandmother would knock the freshly polished knocker against the black door and Mrs Trivett, wrapped in a voluminous apron, would open it, releasing the warm scent from the bubbling concoction, which later would become the sweets I loved.

Taking me into her kitchen she would show me how they were made. Fat strips of the sugary-smelling black and white mixture were placed over a hook by the door, then squeezed and pulled until they trebled in length. Only when their length had increased to Mrs Trivett's satisfaction were they taken down, some to be cut into small squares, others into larger pieces which were rolled into humbugs.

Engrossed, I would watch, my cheeks bulging with some of her samples, as I rolled the one she had told me I could 'test' around my tongue. When the last drop of the sugary syrup had slid down my throat I would play the same game we played every time.

'Mrs Trivett, what are little girls made of?'

I never grew tired of her reply.

'Why Antoinette, how many times do I have to tell you? Sugar and spice, of course, and all things nice!'

I would giggle happily and she would reward me with another sweet.

On other days my mother showed me the games she'd enjoyed playing as a child; the sort of games passed down through the decades, from generation to generation. We dressed dolls and made mud pies with a small bucket and spade. But my favourite one involved using a tea set my grandmother had given me to give pretend tea parties. First I would arrange the tiny cups and saucers on a cloth, beside them the teapot and miniature milk jug. Then the matching plates would be laid in a neat row. When the cloth table was ready to my satisfaction small pebbles or flowers would take the place of sandwiches and cakes, which would then be offered to my adult playmates or my collection of dolls. Imaginary tea would be poured and passed round and dolls' faces wiped clean of invisible crumbs.

Not only did my mother have unlimited time to show me childhood games, she used to love dressing me in pretty clothes, many of which she made herself, taking hours over the hand-stitched smocking which went across the bodice as was the fashion then.

She had a professional photograph taken of me in one of them when I was three, wearing a gingham dress edged in white with one plump leg crossed over the other, smiling confidently into the camera. I looked the loved child I knew I was.

My mother entered me for a 'Miss Pears' competition and to her joy I was one of the runners-up. A small, framed photograph took pride of place on the mantelshelf.

But those happy days, when we were a family of two, were numbered. For years I dreamed of them returning, but over ten years later, when they finally did, they brought no happiness.

My father stayed in the army for several years after the war and only visited us sporadically, stirring the house into an uproar for the short time he was there. To me he seemed more like an important visitor than a parent. Days before his arrival there would be a flurry of housework, cushions would be shaken, furniture polished and floors mopped. A warm smell of baking would fill the house as his favourite biscuits and cakes were made, then, on the long-awaited day, my mother would dress me in my best outfit while her prettiest was donned. Constantly gazing impatiently out of the window, we would wait for the gate to open and a loud greeting to be called, upon which my mother would rush to the door and into his outstretched arms.

My impression was of a big handsome man who made my mother laugh with happiness while a pink glow suffused her face. Presents such as silk stockings for her and chocolate for me always accompanied his arrival. My mother would unwrap hers patiently, meticulously folding the paper for future use, whilst I ripped mine open with squeals of delight. He, the benevolent visitor, would sit in the most comfortable chair and smile at our pleasure.

For my fourth birthday a bulky parcel had been torn open to reveal a large, red, stuffed felt elephant. Picking her up I thought she was more beautiful than any doll. I christened her Jumbo and for several months refused to be parted from her. Holding Jumbo by the trunk I trailed her around the house, insisting she shared my bed and taking her with me on visits.

A few months after that birthday my father announced that the idea of civilian life appealed to him. He wanted, he said, to spend more time with his wife and daughter. When my mother heard those words her face lit up and for the next few weeks I could sense her exhilaration as she waited for him to return, this time to stay.

I knew the day he was expected from the smells of baking and frantic housework, but it was another three days before he finally arrived. This time there were no presents after the shouted greeting and within hours the carefree atmosphere in our home changed for ever. The build-up of tension had begun.

After I was put to bed clutching my much-loved elephant, the first row I'd heard between my parents penetrated my sleep. I felt unsettled. Up to then I'd hardly heard a voice raised in anger. I hugged Jumbo a little tighter, hoping they would stop, and eventually fell uneasily back to sleep.

A long time later my mother told me it was because of my father's drinking and gambling. I knew nothing of the causes; I just knew the result made me uncomfortable. Upon leaving the army with his severance pay he had not returned home until every penny of it had been lost on a poker table and my mother's hopes of buying a house that she could turn into a home for us were dashed. It was clear to me, as she talked in one of the rare intimate moments we had, that it was only the first of many disappointments to come.

My mother realized that with a growing child and no lump sum to fall back on, if she was ever going to achieve her ambition of owning her home, she would have to work. But it wasn't going to be easy. Not only was there no equal pay for women in the decade after the war, there was very little work. Victorious servicemen who had remained in the army to help rebuild a devastated Germany had returned to face massive unemployment, substandard accommodation and rationing. With a grim determination that was an integral part of her character, my mother was never going to admit defeat and eventually her persistence was rewarded. She found employment at a garage several miles away as a night-shift cashier, where a small, dark, rent-free family flat made up part of her wages.

My father also found obtaining work difficult. Although he was a trained mechanic the only position he could find was in a factory, also on night shifts. With no alternative on offer he took it.

Our lives then settled into a different pattern, with him returning home each morning grumbling about tiredness and going straight to bed, whilst my mother, who had a home to run and a small child to look after, snatched sleep whenever she could.

Although my grandmother sometimes arranged to collect me for an outing, she seldom visited us and the days of spending time with my mother alone also came to an end. I would wake up in the little flat, clutch Jumbo for support and go in search of her. Finding the flat empty I would wander down to the garage in my nightclothes, still half asleep, seeking her company. In those early days she never got angry with me, just picked my still sleepy body up, laughed, took me upstairs and tucked me back into bed.

A few months before my fifth birthday we moved again, this time to a small terraced house with a garden. My father had just received a promotion that meant permanent work with more pay and better hours. Night work was tiring for my mother, and now for the first time since her husband's return she felt she could become a full-time housewife.

The night before my birthday I lay awake, wondering what present I would be given. All through the previous week I'd nagged my mother to tell me. Immune to my pleas she laughed and told me I would have to curb my curiosity and wait until the day to find out.

Waking early I rushed downstairs, remembering the arrival of Jumbo a year before, and scanned the sitting room. I couldn't see anything. Seeing the look of disappointment on my face, my mother told me we were going to visit someone, and I would be given my present there.

As soon as I had excitedly gulped my breakfast down I was buttoned into my coat and I skipped along, holding my mother's hand as we made our way to the bus stop. A red double-decker bus took us several miles to the next village. Alighting, we walked a short distance to a house I'd never seen before. I was puzzled. I had no idea what my present could possibly be. Presents, I knew, were bought in shops.

On my mother's knock I heard the shrill barking of several dogs. My excitement mounted. Jumbo, though still much loved, was beginning to lose her attraction for me. What I now wanted more than anything was a puppy of my own. Was this, I wondered, the day my wish was to be granted?

A small, plump, grey-haired woman opened the door. Scampering around her feet were several black-and-tan wirehaired terriers, wagging their tails as they jumped up to welcome us. Trying to quieten their boisterous greeting, she ushered us quickly into a large kitchen. My excitement grew when I saw in front of the stove a basket filled with several sleeping puppies. Just outside it a fluffy little creature, with the black-and-tan markings of the adult dogs and bright mischievous eyes, stumbled around on legs still shaky, sniffing the air with her black button of a nose.

Before my mother had time to ask the lady to show me the others, I'd rushed to the adventurous one and knelt down. I knew instantly she wanted me as her owner. Picking her up, breathing in that warm puppy smell, feeling small quick licks from her rough pink tongue on my face as she wriggled in my arms, the bond was formed; she became the greatest friend of my childhood.

'Is that the one you like the most?' my mother asked.

My radiant face was all the answer she needed.

'Then she's yours. She's your birthday present.'

I gasped with pure pleasure as I realized my greatest wish had just been granted. I kissed the little dog on top of her fluffy black and tan head, and with that display of five-year-old maternal love I showed her she was mine.

'What are you going to call her?' my mother asked.

The memory of another small, determined figure came into my head, a figure I'd seen when I'd spent a magical day at the beach earlier that year. My grandmother had taken me by train to the seaside town of Ramsgate on the Kent coast. Clutching a large ice-cream cone I'd seen a circle of laughing children sitting transfixed in the warm sun, their eyes fixed on something out of my vision. Tugging impatiently at my grandmother's hand to pull her forward, looking in the same direction as the other children, the two figures of Punch and Judy came into view. My forgotten ice cream melted and trickled down my hand as I stood rooted to the spot, enthralled by their antics. I booed when Punch attacked Judy and cheered with the other children when Judy lambasted him back. Even when the puppeteer came round with his collection box the mystery of the two miniature figures remained unexplained and my ever-patient grandmother was subjected to a stream of questions about the fighting dolls.

'I'm going to call her Judy,' I replied.

That birthday was to remain the happiest memory of my childhood.

My mother had enrolled me at a small private school. Each morning she would take me and every afternoon she would be waiting at the school gates with a warm smile. I felt very grown up wearing my uniform, with my pencils, eraser and first learning books carefully placed in a canvas satchel that hung over my shoulder. Even though I liked those early days of learning, I spent most of each day with bated breath, visualizing Judy in my mind, longing for the final bell. I would hurriedly swallow the milk and sandwiches, which would be given to me after I'd changed out of my navy-blue gym tunic. Only when I'd finished both would I be allowed outside to play ball with Judy for an hour. When my mother thought enough energy had been burnt up for us both to settle down quietly she would open the kitchen door and call us in. A reading book, where new words were learnt every day, or a counting one where I was learning to tell the time, would be removed from my satchel. I would work at the table while my mother made supper and Judy lay exhausted at my feet.

For Christmas, when she was turning from puppy to small dog, I used my saved-up pocket money to buy a smart red lead with matching collar. Now, proudly buttoned up in my warm navy winter coat, with Judy prancing beside me impervious to the cold in her natural fur, I would take her for walks, beaming with pleasure every time someone stopped to admire her. My happiness was completed when my grandmother started to visit again. No explanation had ever been given as to why she had stopped. Years later she admitted to me she had been appalled at us living above the garage, had never liked my father and had never thought him good enough for my mother. Whilst by then I more than agreed with her, it was too late to comment.

She, like me, adored Judy, who always greeted her rapturously. My grandmother would pick her up, tickle her stomach and be rewarded by licks that removed her perfumed face powder.

With my grandmother's visits would come presents, mainly of books which, when my mother was busy, my grandmother would always find time to read to me.

When my parents informed me in February that we were

going to move to Northern Ireland, where my father came from, my pleasure was only spoilt by the thought of not being able to see so much of my grandmother. Her many reassurances of numerous visits, however, made my fears disappear.

In fact, six years were to pass before I saw her again.

We sent regular letters, which hid the truth of our family life. She never forgot birthdays and Christmases, but the hoped-for letter announcing a visit never arrived. Unaware then of the many excuses my mother was making to her, my grandmother gradually faded in my life to become someone who had once loved me.

Chapter Three

Three thin wooden tea chests and one suitcase stood on our sitting-room floor, containing the accumulated chattels of a marriage. Over the next ten years I saw them packed and unpacked many times until they became a symbol to me of defeated optimism. At five and a half, however, I saw them as the start of an exciting adventure. My mother had triumphantly nailed the third one shut the preceding night and once a van arrived to collect them our journey was to begin.

My father, who had already been in Northern Ireland for several weeks looking for suitable accommodation, had finally sent for us. His longed-for letter had arrived a week earlier and my mother had read parts out to me. He had, she told me enthusiastically, found a house for us in the country. First, however, we were to visit his family, who were eagerly awaiting our arrival. We would stay with them for a fortnight until our chests and furniture arrived, at which time we would move to our new home.

My mother told me time and again how much I would love Ireland, how it would be a good life and how I would enjoy meeting all my new relatives. She talked excitedly of her future plans; we were going to live in the country, start a poultry farm and grow our own vegetables. Envisioning Easter-card yellow fluffy chicks my enthusiasm grew to match hers. I listened to the extracts of my father's letter that she read out to me about my cousins, about the house in the country and about how much he was missing us. Her happiness was infectious as she described a future idyllic life.

When the van had left with our chests and furniture I looked at our bare rooms with a mixture of emotions: nervous at leaving everything that was familiar, but excited at going to a new country.

My mother picked up our hand luggage and I took a firm hold of Judy's lead as we started our twenty-four-hour journey. What to me seemed like an adventure, to my mother must have felt like a gruelling ordeal. Not only did she have our bags and me to look after, but also Judy, who by now had grown from a puppy into a small, bright-eyed, mischievous terrier.

A bus took us to the railway station, with its tubs of flowers and friendly porters. We caught a train to the Midlands, then the connecting train to Crewe. I sat in the compartment watching the steam floating in smoky clouds back from the engine, listening to the wheels making their clickety-clack clickety-clack noise, which sounded to me like 'we're going to Northern Ireland, we're going to Northern Ireland'.

I could hardly sit still, but the excitement did not curb

my appetite. Mindful of our budget, my mother had packed a picnic for us. Unwrapping the brown-tinged greaseproof paper I found a round of corned beef sandwiches, then a hard-boiled egg, which I peeled and ate as I stared out the window. A crisp apple followed, while my mother poured herself tea from a flask. There was a separate packet containing scraps for Judy, a bottle of water and a small plastic bowl. She ate every crumb, licked my fingers gratefully, and then fell asleep curled at my feet. After we'd finished my mother took a damp cloth from another small bag, wiped my face and hands before taking out a gilt powder compact and swiftly puffing powder onto her nose and chin. Pursing her lips, she painted them the dark red she always favoured.

Crewe station seemed a vast, noisy cavern of a place, dirty and poorly lit, completely unlike the pretty freshly painted stations of Kent. My mother bundled me up in my wool coat, placed Judy's lead in my hand, then organized our bags.

The boat train from Crewe to Liverpool was packed with happy passengers in a holiday mood, many of them servicemen going home on leave. There was no shortage of helping hands to lift our bags onto the rack above our heads. Judy received many pats and compliments, which pleased me. My pretty mother, with her shoulder-length dark hair and trim figure, had to explain to more than one hopeful serviceman that her husband was waiting for us both in Belfast.

With my colouring books and crayons out, not wishing to miss a moment, I desperately tried to keep my eyes open, but to no avail. Within an hour sleep overcame me.

When I awoke we had arrived at Liverpool. Through the swirls of steam I saw the boat for the first time, a huge grey forbidding mass that towered above our heads. It cast a shadow over the scores of people who, carrying an assortment of luggage, were rushing to queue at the base of the gangplank. The weak yellow beams of the streetlights shone dimly on the oily water beneath the gently swaying boat. Having only ever seen the small fishing fleets of Ramsgate, I felt overawed that we were going to travel on something so huge. Holding Judy's lead tightly I moved closer to my mother for comfort as we shuffled forward to join the queue.

Helping hands assisted us aboard where a white-coated steward showed us to our small second-class cabin, furnished with a wooden chair, a single bunk and a small sink.

'What, two of us are going to sleep in there?' I exclaimed in disbelief.

The steward ruffled my hair and laughed. 'Sure, you're not very big!'

That night I cuddled up to my mother as the swell of the sea rocked me to sleep for most of the twelve-hour crossing. I never had the feeling of seasickness that, according to the purser when he brought us our morning tea and toast, so many of our fellow passengers had.

We arrived in Belfast before the sun had fully risen, and queued once more to alight. Passengers were waving as they leant over the side but, being too small, I had to contain my eagerness. As the boat made its final lurch the gangplank was lowered and my first sight of Belfast came into view.

The dawn light shone on damp cobbles, where small ponies pulled wooden traps back and forth. People with freezing breath milled around the gangplank, broad smiles of greeting on their faces. My ears were assailed by the harsh Northern Irish accent as relatives and friends found one another.

Everything looked and sounded so different as we searched for my father. We saw him simultaneously, coming towards us with a huge smile. He hugged my mother tightly as he kissed her, picked me up, swung me into his arms and kissed me loudly on each cheek. Judy sniffed around his feet suspiciously, and for once her tail didn't wag.

He said how much he'd missed us, how pleased he was we were there and how everyone was looking forward to seeing us. Picking up our suitcases, he led the way to a car.

He'd borrowed it, he told us with a wink, for the last stage of our journey. My mother glowed with delight when she heard how he didn't want her to travel to Coleraine by train, wasting precious moments when he could be with us.

With me wrapped up warmly in a tartan rug on the back seat we started the final lap. He held her hand and I heard him say, 'Everything's going to be different, you'll see, we're going to be happy here. It'll be good for Antoinette too, all the country air.' My mother leant her dark head against his shoulder and he rested his auburn one briefly against it. That day their happiness was tangible. Young as I was, I could feel it.

For the first time I felt excluded. My father kept his

attention focused on my mother. I saw her smiles, which today were not for me, and knew they were absorbed in one another. A feeling of apprehension, as if I'd been given a warning of changes to come, settled on me as I watched the unfolding landscape.

I saw the indigo Irish mountains, their peaks still shrouded in early morning mist. Across a rugged landscape squat, grey square houses, so unlike the pretty black and white thatched cottages of Kent, broke up the acres of green. I spotted clusters of sheep huddled together for warmth in fields separated by low flint walls. We passed tiny hamlets where one small house, turned into a general shop, serviced the local community. Pigs with scrawny chickens pecking round their feet snuffled contentedly in the muddy yards of single-storey smallholdings. Children waved at our passing car and, waving back, I held Judy up to the window to see them.

Deciding I liked the look of Ireland, my thoughts turned to my Irish family. Although I loved the maternal grandmother we'd left behind in England, I was looking forward to meeting new relatives. My mother had tried to describe my family to me but I couldn't visualize them. They, I knew, had seen me as a baby, but I had no recollection of them.

The fields were replaced by wide roads with large houses standing in landscaped grounds, which gave way to roads of compact bow-windowed semi-detached homes with their oblong gardens boxed in by neatly clipped hedges. Following them came rows of terraced houses with their flowerless shrubs protected by low walls.

My father told us that we would soon be at his mother's house where lunch would be waiting for us, which reminded me I was hungry. The breakfast of weak tea and toast had been hours before.

A few minutes later all greenery vanished as the streets grew narrower and the houses darker, until we turned into a road of tiny red-brick houses, their front doors opening straight onto the pavements. This, my father told me, was the area where he'd grown up, and where members of my Irish family, including my grandparents, lived. I craned my neck and saw a street completely unlike anything I'd seen before.

Women with headscarves tied over their curlers lent over the tops of their stable front doors, calling across to their neighbours while they watched snotty-nosed toddlers playing in the gutters. Others, bare-legged, feet pushed into carpet slippers, leant against walls inhaling cigarettes through pale lips. Children in ragged clothes played cricket against wickets drawn on walls. Dogs of questionable parentage barked furiously, leaping in the air as they tried to catch balls. Men with braces over their collarless shirts walked aimlessly with their hands in their pockets and caps on their heads, while a few of them standing in a group were having what looked like an intense conversation.

More dogs ran around the car as we parked and climbed wearily out. Not knowing if they were friendly or not I clutched Judy protectively in my arms. She repaid my concern by wagging her tail and wriggling to get down. Waiting to greet us was a short, plump white-haired woman who stood with her hands on her hips and a wide smile on her face.

She seized my father in a fierce hug and then pushed open the door. We stepped past the steep uncarpeted staircase, straight from the pavement into the minute sitting-room of my grandparents' house.

The room was hot with a coal fire blazing brightly and crowded with the immediate members of my father's family. My grandfather looked like a smaller, older version of him. He was a short, stocky man who, like my father, had thick wavy hair swept back from his face. But where my father's waves glinted with dark red lights, Grandfather's had faded into a pale yellowy grey. Like my father he had thickly fringed hazel-grey eyes but when he smiled it was to reveal yellow stained teeth, not the brilliant white gleam of my father's mouth.

My grandmother, an animated little ball of a woman dressed all in black, had white hair done up in a bun and apple-red cheeks beneath twinkling blue eyes. She fussed happily around us and I instantly liked her.

'Antoinette,' she exclaimed, 'I haven't seen you since you were a wee baby, and look at you now, a grown-up girl.'

She pulled forward a young woman, whom she told me was my Aunt Nellie. Petite, with dark hair and brown eyes, she was my father's only sister.

Two more men, whom my father told me were his younger brothers, my uncles Teddy and Sammy, were next to be introduced. They obviously looked up to their big brother. Teddy, a whippet-thin, red-haired teenager with an infectious grin, was a young man impossible to dislike, whilst black-haired Sammy was several years older and more serious looking. Although seeming pleased to see us, Sammy was more restrained in his greeting.

Teddy volunteered to take Judy for a much-needed walk and gratefully I handed over her lead. Feeling shy of my new surroundings, I did not wish to venture out just yet.

My grandmother and Nellie bustled around us, putting food onto the table and pouring boiling water into an aluminium teapot.

'Sit you down, now,' Grandmother said. 'Sure you must be hungry.'

Chairs were hastily pulled up to a laden table and the relatives watched as my grandmother piled my plate high. There was an assortment of sandwiches, some filled with spam or corned beef, others with fish paste. There was brown soda bread and small, thick Irish pancakes spread liberally with butter and strawberry jam. A fruitcake followed, which must have used the whole family's ration budget. I needed no encouragement to eat as I tucked in with gusto, surrounded by the friendly buzz of the adults' conversation as they plied my parents with questions.

When I could eat no more my eyes started closing as the heat of the room, the long journey and the food took their toll. I heard laughing adult voices exclaim that I had fallen asleep, then felt the strong arms of my father as he picked me up and carried me to a bedroom upstairs.

The four o'clock twilight had fallen when my mother woke me. Sleepily, I allowed her to wash and dress me for another visit. It appeared that my entire father's family wanted to see us, and I, used to my mother's small family of one grandmother and a few rarely seen cousins, felt overwhelmed by trying to remember all the names I was hearing. Supper was to be served at my great-uncle's house in the same road. Uncle Eddy and Aunt Lilly, as I was told to call them, and their two teenage daughters, Mattie and Jean, had laid out a special meal for us which, I was to learn, was typical Irish fare: thick slices of chicken, boiled ham coated in the sweet sheen of honey and mustard, hard-boiled eggs, bright red tomatoes and potatoes boiled in their skins. Home-made trifle and numerous cups of tea followed and again I felt the warmth of my father's family wash over me.

They asked about our life in England, how our journey had been and what my parents' plans were now. Where were we going to live? Where was I going to school? I noticed their surprise when my mother informed them I was to be sent to a private school, as that was what I'd been used to. When I was older I realized that only scholarship pupils from Park Street, one of the poorest areas in Coleraine, would have attended the school my mother had chosen for me.

They seldom gave us time to answer their questions before they relayed to us all the family gossip. Even then I could sense my mother was uninterested. I'd come to recognize the polite smile she wore when with company that bored her. In contrast, a cheerful smile rarely left my father's face as he, the centre of attention, laughed at every new item of gossip.

Tired out from the day's excitement, feeling happy that I was part of such a big family, I contentedly slept in a put-you-up bed placed at the foot of my parents' bed.

Daylight filtering through the thin curtains that covered the small window wakened me the following morning. Going in search of my mother I was told my parents had gone out for the day and that I was to stay with my grandmother.

My mother had never left me without telling me first and again I experienced a slight twinge of apprehension and loss. Looking into my new grandmother's kind face, however, I was able to push my doubts aside.

While she made me an 'Ulster fry up', as she called it, of fried pancake, black pudding and egg, I washed myself at the kitchen sink. Going to the outside lavatory I was dismayed to find neatly cut up pieces of newspaper in the place of toilet rolls. When I pointed this out to my grandmother she looked embarrassed and told me they'd just run out and would get some after breakfast. It was not until several months later I realized that poverty gave newspaper several uses and that toilet paper was considered an unnecessary luxury.

Once the breakfast dishes were washed up she boiled more saucepans of water and told me I could help her with the washing. Into the minuscule back yard we went, where a large metal bowl was filled with steaming soapy water. She placed a ridged board into it and proceeded to wash towels and shirts by rubbing them briskly up and down its grooves with hands that were red and chapped, quite unlike my mother's white ones with their carefully applied scarlet nail varnish.

I helped her wring the sodden items through the mangle by holding one end while she fed the other one through, a procedure we repeated several times. When every last drop of water had been wrung out we pegged the washing with fingers already growing numb with cold onto a line suspended between the back door and the lavatory. Finally we hoisted it as high as it could go with the wooden pole that held it in place, letting it float above our heads in the chill air.

Every evening except Sunday the still damp washing would be placed on a wooden clothes horse in front of the fire, filling the room with the smell of steaming clothes and blocking the heat.

Midday brought my grandfather back, not from work as I thought but from the bookies or, if he'd been lucky on the horses, the pub. I was given the task of laying the table, which was covered with clean newspaper, before the meal of soup and soda bread was laid out.

That weekend most of my time was spent with my grandparents while my parents disappeared, not returning until I was already in bed asleep. On Sunday morning my mother saw my woebegone face when I realized she and my father were going out again and promised we would spend the following day together.

'First I'm taking you to be enrolled at your new school,' she said. 'Then, if you're good and stay to help your grandmother today, I'll take you out for lunch as a special treat.'

Placated, I beamed back at her, happy again, and she gave me a quick hug, leaving the smell of her perfume lingering in the air.

Monday brought a weak winter sun that brightened but failed to warm the cold morning. However, anticipation of a whole day with my mother took the chill off it.

'It's only a half hour's walk,' she reassured me.

After breakfast we walked hand in hand out of the narrow streets around Park Street, across the town square and into tree-lined avenues, where tall red-brick houses stood back from the roads. On reaching one that was only distinguished from the nearby houses as a school by its several grey prefab buildings and fenced-in tennis courts, we entered its large wooden-floored hall and introduced ourselves to the school secretary.

Within a few minutes we were shown to the headmistress's rooms. She was an imposing woman; her white hair tinged slightly blue, dressed in a tailored grey suit, which was almost covered by a black gown.

'Hello, I'm Dr Johnston,' she said, touching my shoulder briefly. 'You must be Antoinette.'

After talking to my mother for a few minutes she set me a simple reading test, which I read straight through without stumbling once, despite my nerves. When I'd finished she smiled at me warmly.

'Antoinette, you read very well, even though you've only been at school a few months. Did your mother teach you?'

'No, Nanny taught me,' I replied. 'We used to read Flook cartoons together in the *Daily Mail.*' She laughed and asked what else my grandmother had taught me. She seemed amused when I said that I'd learnt to count by playing cards.

'Well, she's certainly up to standard,' she reassured my mother. 'I think she will fit in well here.'

My mother looked pleased and I was content with her pleasure. After various formalities Dr Johnston gave us a tour around the school. Looking at the groups of children dressed in their green uniforms, playing in their break, I thought I was going to be happy there.

Armed with lists of what was required, my mother and I walked the short distance into town. First we bought my uniform, green gym tunic, three white shirts and a black and green tie. The last purchase, which my mother told me was a present from my English grandmother, was a smart green blazer with its distinctive white badge on the breast pocket. The next stop was the bookshop.

Weighed down by all our parcels, we made our way to a nearby tearoom for the promised treat of lunch.

'I think you're going to like your new school,' my mother said as soon as our food had arrived. With my mouth full of toasted, buttery crumpet I nodded happily in reply.

The morning I was due to start I jumped eagerly out of bed and rushed downstairs to wash and eat the breakfast my grandmother had already cooked for me. My father had left for work and my mother had laid out all my new clothes on their bed. I could smell the newness of them. I dressed myself from my green school knickers to my gym tunic, asking my mother for help with my tie. My hair was brushed, a slide clipped in to hold it into place, then, with my satchel containing all my new books slung across my shoulder, I gave myself a glance in the mirror. A happy child with just a residue of puppy fat smiled confidently back at me. I preened for a moment and then descended the stairs to be hugged by my grandmother before my mother and I left for the walk to school.

My teacher introduced me to my classmates and sat me beside a friendly blonde-haired girl, whom I was told was named Jenny. The morning passed quickly and I gave thanks for my English grandmother's extra tuition. I found the reading and arithmetic easy and was rewarded by a smile and words of praise from my teacher.

At the sound of the bell our class rushed from the schoolroom to the play area where Jenny took me under her wing. Finding my name difficult to pronounce, the children, with peals of laughter, called me 'Annie-net'. Knowing their laughter was friendly I was happy to feel part of this group and laughed with them. By the end of the day Jenny and I had become best friends. She seemed to like the kudos of looking after a little girl with a strange accent and proudly introduced me to my fellow classmates. Basking in her attention I felt the warmth that sudden friendship brings. The need for a best friend that starts when babyhood ends and childhood begins was fulfilled.

Two more weeks passed at my grandparents' house until

the day of our moving came. This time I had mixed feelings; I loved being part of such a big family, especially being the youngest member and the centre of attention. I was constantly fussed and petted by them all. Even my taciturn grandfather would chat to me, send me on errands to the tiny local shop to buy cigarettes for him and sweets for me. When nobody was looking he would even make a fuss of Judy. I knew I was going to miss them, but my adventurous side looked forward to living in the countryside and helping my mother with her poultry farm.

A compromise had been reached to appease both my grandparents and me. It was common then in the rural areas for the buses to run only twice a day, once in the morning to take the workers into town and then in the evening to return them. It was arranged that every school day I would go to my grandparents' house for tea, then they would take me to my bus and my mother would meet me at the other end. Knowing she was not going to see me until after the Easter holidays, my grandmother prepared a food parcel full of my favourite Irish soda breads and pancakes, which we packed into the car along with saucepans, packets of groceries and fuel.

Saying tearful goodbyes to my grandmother, we loaded up the car with our suitcases. Then, with Judy and I tightly squeezed into the back, we started our journey to our new house. Behind us followed a van containing our meagre furniture from England, none of which my mother could bear to part with.

Main roads became country ones, then we drove down a lane where the hedgerows were wilder and gravel replaced the tarmac, until we came to a dirt track leading to double wooden gates.

My father jumped triumphantly from the car, threw open the gates with a flourish and we saw the thatched house for the first time. It was not what I had expected.

Back in the hospice cold touched my skin as the memories churned in my head, and I felt incapable of movement. The hardness of the chair prodded me awake; Antoinette was gone and Toni, my adult self, was back in charge.

I poured myself a vodka from my flask, lit a cigarette and rested my head against the back of the chair to reflect on the happiness of those early years. Why, I wondered, did I feel overcome with feelings of impending doom? There was nothing in this place to scare me.

'Yes there is, Toni,' came the whisper. 'You're scared of me.'

'I'm not,' I retorted. 'You're my past and the past is dealt with.'

But the denial was hollow. As I looked into the corners of the empty room through my cloud of smoke I felt the power of Antoinette drawing me back through the gates to the thatched house.

Chapter Four

In an expanse of gravel liberally studded with dandelions stood a small square house. Peeling white paint exposed grey patches from earlier days and brackish stains ran in streaks from the guttering. There were two water butts held together with rusty iron brackets, a padlocked stable door and four grimy uncurtained windows.

To the side of the house stood two tumbledown sheds with corrugated iron roofs. A tangle of brambles and nettles barred the double doors of the larger one and missing slats left black gaps in the walls. The door of the smaller shed hung open, revealing yellowing squares of newspaper hanging on string and the worn wooden seat of a chemical lavatory. Planks formed a path almost obliterated by brambles and weeds and damp had rotted away the wooden square in front.

My mother, I knew, saw the pretty cottages of Kent. Saw her handsome husband and felt the love for a static memory that was locked into her mind. It was that of a dance hall, where she, older than most of the women there, had been danced off her feet by an auburn-haired charmer to the envy of her friends.

With that picture in her head and her optimism still intact, she started explaining her plans. The large outhouse would be turned into a deep litter barn for chickens, a vegetable garden would be grown at the rear of the house and flowers would be planted underneath the windows. Taking my hand she led me inside.

The draught from the open door sucked the dust balls from their corners. The last struggles of hundreds of trapped flies had ended in the giant dusty cobwebs that looped from unpainted rafters and windows, and a trail of old mouse droppings led to the only built-in cupboard. The walls had been painted white but from the floor to the height of my waist they were speckled with the dark green of damp.

A black peat-fuelled range stood at one end of the room and under a window was the only other fitting, a wooden shelf with a metal bowl on top and a tin bath underneath.

Two doors at opposite ends led into the bedrooms. By the front door a staircase, not much more than a ladder, provided an entrance to the attic. When we climbed up to explore we found a large dark space where only the thatch protected us from the elements, and a damp musty smell made me wrinkle my nose.

My mother set to work on her dream immediately, vigorously sweeping the floors as the men unpacked the van. Peat was brought in; a fire was lit in the stove and water drawn from the well at the bottom of the garden. My first task was to remove all the frogs that came up in the bucket, carrying them carefully back to the grass near the well.

'Then they can choose whether they want to rejoin their families or stay above ground in the sun,' my mother explained.

As warmth seeped from the stove, familiar furniture was arranged around the now cobweb-free room and the battery-driven radio played music my mother could hum along to, a cheerful atmosphere pervaded the previously desolate room.

Tea and sandwiches were prepared and I took mine outside to sit with Judy on the grass. I shared my corned beef sandwich with her while she sniffed the new smells with a twitching nose and her head cocked on one side, giving me a hopeful look.

Kent seemed a world away and I, like her, felt like exploring. Seeing the grown-ups were all busy I put Judy's red lead on and slipped out through the gates. As we strolled up the nearby lane the early spring sun beat down, taking away the lingering chill of the cottage. The unclipped hedgerows were bursting with wild flowers. There were clumps of primroses and early wild honeysuckle. Purple violets peeked out from underneath the white hawthorn. Bending down I picked some to make into a posy for my mother. Time passed unheeded as the new sounds and sights caught my attention and more flowers tempted me to wander further down the lane.

Stopping to watch fat pigs in a nearby field with their plump pink young running alongside, I heard my father shouting, 'Antoinette, where are you?'

I turned around and trotted trustingly towards him, clutching my posy of wild flowers. But the man I saw coming towards me was not the handsome smiling father who'd met us from the boat. In his place strode a scowling, red-faced man I hardly recognized, a man who suddenly appeared huge, with bloodshot eyes and a mouth that trembled with rage. My instinct told me to run but fear kept me rooted to the spot.

He grabbed hold of me by the neck, put his arm tightly around my head and pulled it against his body. He lifted my cotton dress to my waist and wrenched my pants down to meet my cotton socks. One calloused hand held my semi-naked body against his thighs while the other stroked my bare bottom, squeezing one cheek hard. Seconds later I heard a crack and felt a stinging pain. I wriggled and screamed to no avail. One hand tightened its grip around my neck while the other rose and fell time after time. Judy cowered behind me and the posy, now forgotten, lay crushed on the ground.

Nobody had ever hurt me deliberately before. If ever my plump knees had knocked together, making me fall, my mother always picked me up and wiped away my tears. I screamed and cried in pain, disbelief and humiliation. Tears and snot streamed from my eyes and nose as he shook me. My whole body shuddered with terror.

'Don't you ever go wandering off like that, my girl,' he shouted. 'Now get back to your mother.'

As I pulled my knickers up over my stinging bottom, the

choking tears making me hiccup, his hand gripped my shoulder and he dragged me home. I knew my mother had heard my screams, but she said nothing.

That day I learnt to fear him, but it was another year before the nightmare started.

The second Easter had arrived at the thatched house and the bitter cold of our first winter was almost forgotten. The barn had been repaired, incubators installed in what had been my bedroom and I, against my wishes, had been moved to the attic.

Our original chickens, which my mother saw more as pets than income, scratched happily in the grass outside. The cockerel strutted in front of his harem, proudly displaying his brilliantly coloured plumage, and the incubators were filled with eggs. Unfortunately, numberless rabbits had helped themselves many times to the flowers hopefully planted beneath the windows, and potatoes and carrots were the only survivors of the vegetable patch.

Holidays, now that I was twelve months older, brought more household jobs such as using a strainer to remove frogs from water buckets, collecting kindling for the stove and searching for eggs. Unwilling to use the coops provided, the free-range chickens hid their nests in far corners, some in our yard, others tucked away under bushes in the adjoining fields. The deep litter barn housed the majority of them, and every day baskets would be filled ready for the grocer's twice-weekly visits, when he bought our eggs and provided us with groceries.

Each morning I was sent to the local farmer to collect milk that came in metal cans; those were the days before people worried about pasteurization. Each day the farmer's wife would invite me into her warm kitchen and give me milky tea and warm soda bread before I headed home.

During the days I was too busy to worry about the changing atmosphere in our home. The apprehension I'd felt a year ago had become a reality. My mother's happiness was controlled by her husband's moods. Without public transport, with no control over money and not even a public phone within walking distance, the happy woman who once sat laughing in Kent teashops seemed a distant memory. Only Judy and a very tattered Jumbo remained as reminders of those days.

Once dusk fell I would sit reading my books in the orange light of the Tilly lamps, while my mother waited for my father to come home. I would sit quietly, hoping that quietness made me invisible.

Some evenings before I went to bed his car could be heard as it drove into our gravel yard. Then she would leap up, placing the kettle on the stove, putting his previously prepared dinner on a plate and a smile of welcome on her face. Butterflies would knot my stomach as I wondered which father would appear at the door. Would it be the cheerful jovial one flourishing a box of chocolates for my mother and chucking me under the chin? Or the scowling man I'd first seen in the lane and who had appeared more and more frequently after that?

The former could change into the latter at any imaginary slight. My mere presence, I knew, annoyed him. I could feel his gaze on me as I kept my eyes glued to my book, feeling the silent tension build up.

'Can you not help your mother more?' was a question he would put to me repeatedly.

'What are you reading now?' was another.

My mother, still in love with the handsome man who had met us at the docks, was oblivious to my plight. If I put any questions to her in the daytime, as to why my father was often so angry with me, she just told me to try and please him more.

On the nights when the car had not returned before I went to bed my mother's brightness would fade and I would be awoken in the middle of the night by raised voices. The arguing would continue until his drunken shouts finally subdued her. The mornings following these nights would be strained as my mother silently went about the house and I made any excuse to leave it. Those nights were frequently followed by the return of the jovial father the next day, bringing sweets home for me and asking how his 'wee girl' was. He would hand flowers or chocolates to my mother, kissing her on the cheek, bringing her momentary happiness.

I came to dread weekends. Every Friday my mother would wait for her husband, who seldom appeared, and I would be awakened by their rows, indistinguishable words of anger invading my room, fear binding me to my bed as I burrowed under the blankets, trying to escape the ugly sounds.

Every Saturday morning, lying in bed with a self-inflicted

headache, he would command my mother to send me into his room with cups of tea. Tight lipped, she would obey, restricting me to staying near the house. Visits to the farmhouse to collect the milk were now monitored; no more cups of milky tea and warm buttered bread with the friendly farmer's wife.

I seemed to be a magnet for his anger. After one of my visits to the farm I returned with a bantam hen.

'You can take that back, my girl,' were his first words on seeing her.

For once my mother took my side.

'Oh, let her keep her, Paddy,' she cajoled, using her pet name for him. 'She can go outside with the other hens, and Antoinette can have her eggs.'

He snorted but said no more and 'June' the little bantam became my pet. She seemed to know she was special for nearly every morning she came inside to lay my breakfast egg.

Easter gave my father time off from work, and my mother, I know, was hoping for a day out in the car. We sat on Easter Friday waiting for him, me with nervous flutters in my stomach and my mother with a look of hope on her face. When she heard the scrunch of gravel her face lit up. The jovial father entered, and kissed her on the cheek. A box containing an Easter egg was given to me, a box of assorted chocolates for her.

'I've made a special meal,' she told him. 'I'll just lock up the chickens and then I'll serve it up.'

Humming happily under her breath she left the room, leaving us together.

Knowing his mood swings I glanced warily in his direction, but for once he was smiling.

'Come here Antoinette,' he commanded, patting the cushion beside him.

His arm encircled my waist, drawing me onto the settee. Then I felt his arm around my shoulder as he pulled me closer. Craving his affection I snuggled up to him. Could it be, I wondered hopefully, that he has stopped being angry with me?

Sensations of being protected and safe swept over me as I cuddled closer, feeling so happy that his affection towards me had at last reappeared. He stroked my hair.

'You're my pretty little girl, Antoinette,' he murmured as his other hand started caressing my back. Like a small animal I snuggled even closer. 'Do you love your daddy?'

All memories of his temper left me as, for the first time in months, I felt loved by him. I nodded happily. The hand on my back slid lower, then moved gently to the top of my legs. It ran down to the hem of my skirt and I felt the same calloused palm that only a year ago had spanked me viciously, sliding over my knee. My body stiffened. One hand tightened on top of my head so I couldn't move, while the other slid across my face and gripped my chin. His mouth came down on mine. His tongue forced its way through my lips. I felt slobber run down my chin and the smell of stale whiskey and cigarette breath filled my nostrils. My feelings of safety left me for ever, replaced by revulsion and fear. He released me abruptly, held me by the shoulders and glared into my face.

'Don't tell Mummy,' he said, giving me a slight shake. 'This is our secret, Antoinette, do you hear me?'

'Yes, Daddy,' I whispered. 'I won't tell.'

But I did. I felt secure in my mother's love. I loved her and she, I knew, loved me. She would tell him to stop.

She didn't.

Chapter Five

My eyes blinked as I forced my brain back into the present and into the hospice. I unscrewed the flask once more, poured myself the last of the vodka and lit another cigarette.

'Now do you remember?' Antoinette whispered. 'Do you really believe your mother loved you?'

'She did,' I protested weakly.

'But she loved him more,' came the reply.

Trying to dam the floodgates as the memories struggled to get through, I took a deep swallow of vodka and inhaled my nicotine sedative.

Through the haze Antoinette held up an unwanted picture; the focus was too sharp for me to be able to force it away with pure willpower.

As though it were yesterday, I saw the room inside the thatched house with two people in it. A woman was sitting on a chintz-covered settee with a small child standing, facing her. With clenched fists and imploring eyes the child drew on all her reserves for the confrontation and searched for the words to describe an adult act.

It was the week after that kiss. Antoinette had waited until her father had returned to work and she and her mother were alone. I saw her still trusting in that mother's love but fumbling for the right words to explain an act that was foreign to her. Her nerviness showed in the way she stood and the mother's anger grew more visible with each word that passed her lips. Faithful little Judy, sensing something wrong, was standing by the child's side with her face looking upwards, her eyes full of canine concern.

Again I felt that blaze of anger flashing from the mother's dark green eyes. This time, through my own adult's eyes, I could sense another emotion lurking behind it. Looking back in time I searched the picture for a clue as to what it might be, and then I saw it. It was fear. She was frightened of what she was about to hear.

Antoinette, at six and a half, only saw the anger. Her slight shoulders sagged, expressions of bewilderment and hurt flitted across her face as her last hope of safety left her. Her mother did not intend to protect her from this.

I heard again the mother's voice commanding her to, 'Never, never speak of it again, will you?'

I heard her reply, 'No, Mummy.'

Her training had started; her silence was assured and the road forward for what was to follow had been successfully cleared.

'You see, you did tell her, you did,' my tormenter whispered.

For years I'd blocked out the picture of my mother being told. I'd forced it to fade from my mind. I had forced Antoinette, the frightened child, to disappear and with her she took my memories. I realized, with a sad acceptance, that my mother had always known what my father felt towards me. How else could the child have described that kiss, if she hadn't actually experienced it? She couldn't possibly have invented it. Out in the country in those days there was no exposure to television, she had no books or magazines that could have allowed her to learn about such things. My mother had heard only the truth from her child.

'Remember our last year, Toni,' Antoinette asked, 'the year before you left me? Look at this picture.'

She slid another memory into the receptacle of my mind. It showed my father coming home from prison eleven years later. How my mother had sat looking out of the window waiting for him. Seeing him in the distance, only then had her face come to life as she rushed to meet him.

'You were forgotten then. She never forgave you, but she forgave him.'

Still I did not want to accept the memories that were being set free in my head. I had realized a long time ago that my mother's recollection had stayed for ever locked onto the picture of the handsome, charming man of her youth. She, five years older than him and cursed with a beautiful mother, remained in her own mind the plain woman, lucky to have such a man.

'And nothing or nobody would take him away,' Antoinette retorted. 'Think of the last months at the thatched house, and think about what she finally did.'

Could she, I wondered that night, have loved him so much that she committed the ultimate betrayal to keep him?

Another cigarette was lit as I wondered if any of my questions would ever be answered, any explanation given, or had she lived in the state of denial for so long that her truth had also been firmly buried?

Feeling tiredness almost swamp me, I closed my eyes briefly and, half asleep, I returned to the thatched house.

A steady stream of almost imperceptible changes over the passage of two years had gradually unwoven the fabric of my life. For comfort I would try and conjure up the face of my English grandmother and the memories of feeling secure and loved when I was around her. I would remember when just my mother and I had lived together, days when she had played with me, days when she had read my favourite stories at bedtime and days of just feeling happy.

In bed at night, feeling knots of despair growing in my stomach, I tried to cling onto those elusive memories, to hold onto the feeling of warmth that they gave, but each day they slipped further and further out of reach.

A distance had sprung up between my mother and me, a cold space that I could not breach. Gone were the days when for a surprise she would arrange for a neighbour to drive her into town so that she could meet me from school. Gone were the days when she would listen to my chatter with a smile on her face, and gone were the days when she spent hours making me pretty clothes. In the place of my loving, laughing mother a stranger had appeared, gradually invading her body until the mother I'd known was no longer there, a stranger who had little time for me. Not understanding what I'd done wrong, I felt increasingly bewildered, unhappy and alone.

At the start of the summer holidays I realized that my visits to my grandparents were to come to an end when my mother informed me I was not going back to my junior school in the town. She had enrolled me in the local village school, which was four miles away.

I couldn't stop the tears coming to my eyes, but I furiously blinked them away, having already learnt not to show any weakness. Instead of crying in front of her, I took Judy for a walk and once out of sight let the tears fall. Not to see my best friend again, not to be part of the school I thought I would stay at for years, and never to see my grandparents alone and have the teasing conversations with my relatives that I had been enjoying so much. The prospect was too bleak to be bearable.

I learnt the meaning of isolation that summer and a feeling I was too young to put a name to entered my head: it was the feeling of betrayal.

September came and another first day at a new school began, a few days before my seventh birthday. This time there was no excitement in me as I dressed in my old school uniform and prepared myself for the first of many long walks. Not only was there very little public transport in those days, there was no school bus either. I could remember other first days and my mother taking me when it was only a short distance. Now I was to do the daily four-mile walk to school and the walk back alone.

The first time the road seemed to stretch endlessly into the distance, with only a few scattered cottages breaking up the scenery, which that day gave me no pleasure. As I trudged along for over an hour, I was quite surprised I was able to find the school at all. Other pupils were arriving on bicycles and on foot and for the first time I realized that the school was mixed. Up till then I'd been used to a girls-only school. Squaring my shoulders for the challenges that lay ahead, I walked in and went in search of a teacher.

The school building was completely unlike the mellow red-bricked one I was used to. It was a low, grey, utilitarian building, divided into two classrooms, one for the under eights and the other for children between eight and eleven. Here, when we had our breaks there was no grass to play on; instead a concrete playground was deemed sufficient for the needs of the hundred or so children who attended.

At this school, when the breaks came, there was no Jenny to introduce me around, no companionable laughter that drew me in to feel part of their group; instead clusters of children dressed in a different uniform stared at me with open suspicion.

The pupils, mainly local farm-labourers' children, sniggered at my English accent and my old private school uniform which, since it was not worn out, my parents had insisted I wore, while the teachers ignored me.

Lunchtime came and groups or pairs of noisy children ran to the small canteen, everyone busy saving places for their friends. Confused, I looked around for a seat. Spotting one at the end of the table I placed my satchel on the chair before joining the queue for food. Mashed potatoes with corned beef and stewed cabbage was served and as I forced it down in silence I knew I had entered a different world, one where I was no longer 'Annie-net' but an alien to those around me. Pride kept me quiet as the children mocked me with an undercurrent of aggression, which over the years I would become familiar with but which was then still an unknown quantity.

That year, as the seasons changed from summer to autumn and the evenings drew in, bringing with them an eerie twilight dusk, my four-mile walk home seemed to take longer every day. The hedgerows and trees cast sinister shadows, turning what had been a pretty walk into a frightening journey.

Gradually my fear of the dark grew and twilight with its shadows became an enemy. I would try and walk faster but my school satchel, crammed with sharpened pencils, reading and arithmetic books, seemed to get heavier with each step I took. The middle of October, when the clocks turned afternoons into evenings, brought winds that took the leaves from the trees. In November I encountered another enemy, the rain. With my head down I would struggle through every downpour, knowing that in the morning my coat would still be damp. The water would soak through to my gym tunic and over the weeks the creases gradually disappeared until the smart confident girl I had been only a few months before had disappeared. When I looked in the mirror I saw in her place an unkempt child, whose puppy fat had melted from her bones. A child dressed in crumpled clothes with lank shoulder-length hair, a child who looked uncared for, a child whose face showed a stoic acceptance of the changes in her life.

Half-way between the school and the thatched house was a shop, which like many of the buildings scattered nearby was designed to withstand the bleak Irish weather, not to enhance the countryside. It was a squat stone building with a concrete floor and a simple wooden counter, behind which were numerous shelves. It stocked an extensive array of goods that the local farmers and their labourers needed; everything from oil for the lamps to delicious-smelling home-baked soda breads and locally cured hams.

Here women would come not just for the necessities of life, but for a brief respite from their men folk, and to enjoy a few minutes of female company. With no public transport, limited electricity and in many cases such as ours not even running water, the days were long and hard for the women. They seldom seemed to leave their homes except on

Sundays, where the community of staunch Protestants rarely missed a church service.

The owner of the shop, a kindly woman, would always welcome me with a warm smile. The moment I saw the shop I would quicken my pace, because there I could escape from the cold and find some friendly company. They would sit me down, give me diluted orange squash and sometimes even present me with a scone fresh from the stove, dripping with melting butter. The friendliness of the owner after the bleakness of the school day would warm me and the second half of my journey home would pass more comfortably.

On one of those rare days when the winter sun banishes the shadows of twilight, a small black and white dog, which looked like a miniature Collie, was tied up near the counter. With her matted coat and a piece of rope around her neck she looked as unkempt and in need of love as I did. When I bent down to stroke her she cowered away with a whimper.

'My son rescued her from her previous owner,' the shopkeeper told me. 'She'd been kicked, beaten and even stuffed down a lavatory, poor thing. I'd like to kick them some, being cruel to a wee dog. What sort of people would do that? I need to find a good home for her. I'm sure she just needs some love.'

She gave me a hopeful look.

I felt a warm lick on my hand and, kneeling, I laid my head against the silky black and white one. I knew what it was to need love, and a wave of protectiveness rose in me as I gently stroked her. Five minutes later, after scones and squash, I was walking up the country road holding a rope with the newly named Sally on the other end. That day the rest of my journey home seemed a great deal brighter. Warm licks rewarded me on the frequent stops to reassure Sally that nobody would ever hurt her again, that I would love her and that Judy would be her friend from now on. With that instinctive trust that dogs have, she seemed to know she'd found her protector because her tail came up and her walk quickened.

By the time I turned into our lane the orange light from the Tilly lamp was already glowing and I pushed open the gate and walked to our front door.

'What have we here?' my mother exclaimed as she bent down to pat my new friend. I told her what the shopkeeper had said.

'I can keep her, can't I?' I implored.

'Well, we can't send her back now can we?' was her answer.

I knew that nothing else needed to be said for she was already petting her.

'The poor little thing,' my mother cooed.

To my surprise I saw a film of moisture form in her eyes. 'How can people be so cruel?'

Too young to see the irony in what she said, I just knew Sally had found a new home.

Judy came up, her tail wagging, and curiously sniffed the new arrival with what looked like a friendly greeting to me. It was as though she, a naturally territorial animal, sensed that Sally was no threat to her. She immediately decided to accept her as a four-legged playmate and a new member of the family.

The following morning, to my relief, the jovial father appeared and to my surprise he seemed quite taken with the little dog who, desperate for affection, unlike Judy, gazed at him adoringly.

Now, on my breaks at the shop, I kept the owner informed of Sally's antics, of how she and Judy had bonded, and even told her about June. On hearing, a few weeks later, that the chickens hid their eggs in the overgrown grass at the base of the hedges, she offered me a small goat.

'Antoinette,' she told me, 'take this to your mother. There's nothing better for keeping the grass down.'

Proudly I attached the small animal to a piece of rope, thinking that now we could have goat's milk as well as less grass, and took it home, presenting it as a gift to my mother.

'Now we can get milk,' I told her as the two dogs looked at my new friend with disdain, barked a couple of times and walked off.

'It's a billy goat dear,' she said, with a burst of laughter. 'There's no milk from them. This time you have to take him back.'

The following morning the little goat trotted beside me once more, giving me company for the first two miles of the journey as I walked back to the shop to return him. By that time I felt a sense of relief at handing him back, after my mother had explained how large his horns would grow and the harm he would be able to do with them.

Over those winter months there were moments of genuine warmth between my mother and me and I treasured them, because it was clear that overall her attitude towards me had inexplicably changed. Where once she had taken a pride in my appearance, dressing me in pretty clothes, washing my hair regularly, tying it back with ribbons, her interest in my appearance had almost ceased. I was rapidly growing out of my school uniform; my tunic was several inches above my knees and my jumper, which barely reached my waist, was growing threadbare at the elbows. The pleats in my uniform had now almost disappeared, leaving creases in their place, and the dark green had become shiny, adding to my grubby, uncared-for appearance. My hair, which once my mother had brushed lovingly every day, had now grown straight and lank. The curls of babyhood had long gone, to be replaced by an untidy shoulder-length curtain, framing a face that seldom smiled.

In these times, teachers would have spoken to my mother, but in the 1950s they took out their displeasure on the child.

One young teacher, taking pity on me, tried to be kind. She brought some pretty yellow ribbon in to the classroom and in the break brushed and tied my hair back, holding up a small mirror so I could admire my reflection.

'Antoinette,' she said, 'tell your mother to do your hair like this each day. It makes you look so pretty.'

For the first time in several months I felt I was pretty, and excitedly showed off my new appearance to my mother. Her anger seemed to appear from nowhere as she snatched the ribbon from my hair.

'Tell your teacher that I can dress my own child,' she said, obviously furious.

I was bewildered. What had I done wrong? I asked, but I received no answer.

The next day my hair hung in its usual untidy style and was spotted by the teacher.

'Antoinette, where is the ribbon I gave you?'

Feeling that I would be letting my mother down in some way if I repeated her words, I stared at my feet. A silence fell as she waited for my answer.

'I've lost it.' I heard myself mumble, feeling my face flush from the untruth. I knew I appeared ungrateful and sulky to her, and felt her annoyance.

'Well, at least tidy yourself up, child,' she snapped, and I lost my one ally at that school because it was the last time she bothered to show me any kindness.

I knew I was unpopular amongst my peers, as well as with the teachers. I also knew, young as I was, that the dislike was caused not only by the way I spoke, but also by my appearance. I noticed how differently the other girls looked to me from under their neat, shiny haircuts. Some had slides holding their hair in place, others had theirs tied back with ribbon. Only I had it falling in an untidy mess. Their school uniforms were neatly ironed, their shirts crisp and white and their jumpers were free of darns. Other children who lived several miles from school had bicycles, so their shoes had not become scuffed by the continuous damp that had removed all the shine from mine.

I resolved to do something about my appearance. Maybe then, I thought, I would be more popular.

Summoning up all my courage, I waited until I was alone with my mother to broach the subject of how I could look smarter. That evening, when I got home from school I nervously broached the subject.

'Mummy, can I iron my gym tunic? It needs some of the pleats put back in it. Can I borrow some of Daddy's shoe polish? Can I wash my hair tonight? I'd like to go to school looking smarter.'

One after another my requests tumbled out of my mouth into a silence that became more strained with every syllable I uttered.

'Have you quite finished, Antoinette?' she asked in the cold voice I had come to know so well.

I looked up at her then and, with a sinking heart, recognized the anger in her face. The anger I had seen in her eyes when I had first tried to tell her about my father's kiss had returned.

'Why do you always have to make such a fuss?' she asked, her voice almost a hiss. 'Why do you always have to cause trouble? There is nothing wrong with the way you look; you always were a vain little girl.'

I knew then that any chance I had of being accepted by improving my appearance had gone, and I knew my mother well enough not to argue. Disagreeing with her would result in the one punishment I could not endure, that of being completely ignored.

Every day, as I walked to school with my hands and feet equally cold, I dreaded the day ahead – the unfriendliness of the children, the thinly veiled contempt of the teachers – and I searched my brain for a way of making them like me.

My homework was always meticulously done, my marks high, but somehow I knew that only added to my unpopularity. I noticed that on our breaks other children would have sweets, fruit pastels or sticky toffees. Sometimes these were swapped for marbles, always they were coveted as bargaining tools. Sweets I knew were something children liked, but how could I buy any with no pocket money? Then I saw my opportunity. Once a week the teacher collected the school-dinner money from both classrooms and placed it in a tin box, which she left on her desk. I hatched a plan.

I waited for the other children to leave, quickly went up to the desk, opened the box and took as much of the money as I could stuff into my baggy, elastic-legged knickers. For the rest of that day I walked cautiously around the school, feeling the coins pressing against my skin, reminding me of my guilt. I dreaded that their clinking would reveal me as the thief, but felt jubilant at the success of my plan.

Naturally, once the theft was discovered, our whole class was interrogated and our satchels were searched. Nobody, however, seemed to think of doing a strip search.

I was a very quiet child, because I was very depressed. I appeared well behaved on the surface, but nobody took any interest in how I was feeling underneath. As a result I was the last child to be suspected. When I went home that night I buried the money in the garden. A few days later I dug up a small amount of change, with which I bought a bag of sweets from the village shop on the way to school.

Sidling up to other children in the playground with an uncertain smile on my face, I stretched my arm out with the bag, offering them around. I was immediately surrounded. Hands dipped into my bag, children jostled each other as they eagerly snatched my offerings. I stood in the centre of the group, hearing them laughing and feeling for the first time that I was part of them. A wave of happiness hit me as I felt finally accepted. Then my bag was empty, the last sweet was gone. The laughter, I realized, was at me as the children melted away with whoops of glee as quickly as they had appeared.

I knew then that although they liked the sweets, they were never going to like me. After that day they liked me less for they could sense how desperately I wanted their approval and despised me for it.

I remembered then the visits to Mrs Trivett's house and the question I would always put to her: 'What are little girls made of?' I remembered her reply, and thought now that I must be made of a different substance.

Chapter Six

I would always be exhausted by the time I had walked home, but I still had homework to do. I would sit at the table in our kitchen, which also doubled as our sitting room, trying desperately to stay awake. The only heat came from the cooking range at the far end of the room, the only light from the oil-fuelled Tilly lamps, which gave out a dim, orangey glow.

Once my homework was finished, I would try to sit closer to the warmth of the range and read, or I would watch my mother put a griddle pan onto the stove. Onto it she poured a batter mixture, which magically turned into drop scones or soda bread. We had to be as self-sufficient as possible in those days. Bought cakes and bread were considered to be as great a luxury as red meat or fresh fruit. If it was not home grown we simply didn't buy it.

We had our chickens, which not only provided us with a regular source of eggs but also paid in part for the groceries we bought from the twice-weekly van. Potatoes and carrots were supplied from our vegetable patch, and when I went to the neighbouring farm to collect milk I also collected the buttermilk that my mother used for baking.

Now that I was seven and a half I could read fluently and, during the time we spent at the thatched house, my love for books grew. A mobile library would come at the weekends and I could choose whichever books I wanted. Apart from my animals, books were my escape. I could disappear into other worlds of fantasy, adventure and fun. I could play detective with Enid Blyton's 'Famous Five', explore the underwater world of the *Water Babies* and feel frightened by *Grimm's Fairy Tales. Little Women* showed me how women could be independent. I dreamt of being like Jo when I grew up. Under the light of the Tilly lamps I could have secret adventures with imaginary friends and vanish with them into a life where I was beautifully dressed and where everyone liked me. As my love of reading grew, so did my father's resentment of it.

He never read more than the sports section in the newspaper and considered my mother's and my interest in books a waste of time. Whereas he didn't dare criticize her, he had no qualms in venting his displeasure on me.

'What are you doing that for?' he'd grumble. 'Can you not find something better to do? Does your mother not need you to help? See if there is some washing up to do.'

Another time he'd say, 'What about your homework?'

When I replied, 'I've finished it,' he'd give a disdainful grunt. Unnerved, I would feel his resentment wash over me and pray for bedtime so that I could make my escape.

Full of resentment for anybody who might be happy or educated, my father's rages and tempers were unpredictable. There were the times when he came home quite early, bringing my mother and me sweets and chocolates. Those were the evenings when the jovial father would appear with hugs for my mother and friendly greetings for me. In my mind I had two fathers, the nasty one and the nice one. The nasty one I was very scared of, while the nice one, whom I remembered meeting us at the docks, was the laughing, good-humoured man whom my mother loved. I was only ever allowed rare glimpses of the nice father now, but always hoped for more.

In the spring my father rented a wooden barn, which he said he could keep all his tools in, so that he could repair the car. Housing the chickens, he said, had taken up all the available sheds near the house. This would save us money, he said, since he was a qualified mechanic. Wouldn't it be stupid to be paying other men good money for a job he could do better himself?

My mother agreed with him, which put him in a good humour and suddenly his manner towards me changed. He stopped always being cross, criticizing everything I did. From alternating between wanting me out of the way, ignoring me or shouting at me, he suddenly became friendly all the time. Remembering his hasty fumbles that time when my mother was out of the room, I viewed his overtures with suspicion, but I forced my doubts to one side because, above everything else, I had a desperate need to be loved by my parents. I should have trusted my instincts.

'She's done so much homework this week,' he said to my mother one evening. 'She's had all those long walks to school and back, I'll take her out for a drive in the car.'

My mother smiled brightly. 'Yes, Antoinette, run along with Daddy. He's going to take you out for a drive.'

I jumped into the car enthusiastically, my pleasure only marred when Judy was barred from coming with us. As I sat gazing out of the window I wondered where the drive would take us. I was soon to find out. At the end of our lane he turned off into the field where the small wooden barn he had rented stood. This was where all my weekend drives would lead.

He drove into the dim, shadowy building. The only natural light came from a small window with sacking nailed across it. I felt a sick sensation in the pit of my stomach, felt an unknown fear and knew that I did not want to get out of the car.

'Daddy,' I pleaded, 'please take me home, I don't like it here.'

He just looked at me, with a smile that did not reach his eyes.

'Stay here, Antoinette,' he commanded. 'Your Daddy has a present for you. You're going to like it, you'll see.'

The fear I had of him intensified into terror, creating a leaden weight of dread that kept me firmly in my seat. He got out of the car to lock the shed, then opened the passenger door. When he pulled me round to face him I saw that his trousers were unzipped. His face was red; his eyes were glazed. As I looked into them he no longer seemed to see me. A tremor started deep inside me, shaking my body and forcing its way out of my throat as a whimper.

'You be a good girl now,' he said, taking my child-sized hand, small, plump and dimpled, in his. Holding it firmly, he forced my fingers round his penis then moved them up and down. All the time I was doing it I could hear small animal whimpers escaping from my throat and mingling with his grunts. I shut my eyes tightly, hoping that if I couldn't see then it would stop, but it didn't.

Suddenly my hand was released and my body thrown back across the seat. I felt one hand holding me firmly by pressing on my stomach while another pulled my dress up and yanked my knickers down. I felt shame as my small body was exposed to his eyes and I was pushed further down on the cold leather seat. He pulled me sideways, leaving my legs dangling helplessly over the edge. Legs that I tried in vain to close. I felt him force them further apart, knew he was gazing at the part of me that I thought private, felt a cushion slide under my bottom and then the pain as he pushed himself into me, not hard enough in those early days to tear or damage, but hard enough to hurt.

I lay as limp and as mute as a rag doll, trying to focus on anything apart from what was happening, while the smell of the shed with its combination of damp, oil and petrol, mingled with my father's male smell of tobacco and stale body odour, seemed to seep into the very pores of my skin.

After what seemed like an eternity, he gave a groan and pulled out of me. I felt a warm, wet, sticky substance dripping onto my stomach. He threw a piece of sacking at me.

'Clean yourself up with that.'

Wordlessly, I did as he instructed.

His next words were destined to become a regular refrain: 'Don't you be telling your mother, my girl. This is our secret. If you tell her, she won't believe you. She won't love you any longer.'

I already knew that was true.

The one secret I held back from my father was the secret I held back from myself. My mother did know. The one fear he had was that she would find out. So that was the day we started the game; the game was called 'our secret', a game that he and I were to play for seven more years.

Chapter Seven

My eighth birthday arrived, bringing with it an early autumn quickly followed by the chill of winter. A diet of dark-brown peat was constantly supplied to the stove, producing a red glow, but however much we fed it the warm pool of heat never seemed to spread more than a few feet. I would huddle as close to it as possible as my permanently damp coat, shoes and woollen tights steamed on the wooden clothes horse. Since I only had one of each they had to be ready for the following day.

My mother's voice would float up the still uncarpeted stairs to wake me in the darkness of every early morning, and a chill would nip the tip of my nose as it ventured outside the cocoon of blankets. Automatically my arm would stretch out to the wooden chair, which doubled up as table and wardrobe, as I fumbled for clothes, which I would draw in under the blankets. First my school knickers, followed by woollen tights, brought from the kitchen the night before, were wriggled into. Then, with chattering teeth, my unbuttoned pyjama top would be hastily pulled over my head to be replaced by a woollen vest. Only then would I swing my legs out of bed, leaving my warm nest behind and venturing into the cold of the unheated house. Hastily I would boil the kettle on the range, which would eventually, with some prodding from the poker and some small pieces of peat, come slowly to life.

I would wash quickly at the kitchen sink while my breakfast egg was cooked, then scramble into the rest of my clothes. Breakfast would be consumed hurriedly, then, pulling on my still damp coat, I would pick up my satchel and leave for school.

At the weekends, dressed in an old sweater, mittens and wellington boots, I would help my mother collect eggs, both from the deep litter outhouses and from the scattered hiding places of the free-range chickens. Hoping for brown eggs, she gave them cocoa every morning at eleven o'clock. Whether it increased the ratio of brown eggs to white we were never sure, but the chickens would come running when she called. Greedily, their beaks would dip into the warm sweet liquid time and again. Lifting their heads from the bowls they would shake them, their little beady eyes gleaming as the liquid trickled down their throats.

Frogs would be rescued from the well's bucket and twigs collected for kindling. But my favourite time was when my mother baked. Scones and soda bread were removed from the griddle and, once cooled, placed into tin containers, because food had to be protected from the army of mice that took shelter with us during the winter months.

Sugary-smelling cakes and biscuits were placed onto racks and, if my mother was in a good mood, I would be rewarded with the bowl to lick out, my fingers sliding around its cream and white sides, scrupulously gathering up the last drop of the buttery mixture. I would suck them clean, under the gaze of Judy's and Sally's bright and hopeful eyes.

Those were the days when flashes of the old warmth that kept my love fuelled sprung up between my mother and me. For if her mind was firmly locked on the memory of the handsome auburn-haired Irishman in that dance hall, the man who waited for her at the docks, a man generous with his hugs and unfulfilled promises, mine was for ever locked on the smiling loving mother from my early childhood.

From the money that I'd stolen, I bought myself a torch and batteries. These I hid in my room and at night I would smuggle up a book. Tucked up in bed with the blankets pulled high I would strain my eyes every night as I shone the weak light of the torch onto the print. The rustling and scurrying sounds of the insects and small animals that lived in the thatch receded once I lost myself in the pages. Then for a short time I was able to forget the days when my father took me for the 'drives'.

Each time he picked up his car keys and announced that it was time for my treat I silently implored my mother to say no, to tell him she needed me for an errand, to collect the eggs, fish the frogs out of the well water, even bringing in the water for washing from the rain butts, but she never did.

'Run along with Daddy, darling, while I make tea,' would be her weekly refrain as he drove me to the wooden shed and I learnt to separate my feelings from reality.

On our return sandwiches would have been prepared and a homemade cake, cut into thick slices, would be arranged on a lace doily, which covered a silver-plated platter.

'Wash your hands, Antoinette,' she would instruct me before we sat down to our Sunday afternoon tea.

She never asked me about the drives, never asked where we had been or what we had seen.

Visits to Coleraine, once taken for granted, now became longed-for treats. I missed my large family there, the warmth I always felt in my grandparents' house and the companionship of my cousins.

On the rare occasions my father decided that a visit was due, the tin bath would be filled in a curtained-off part of the kitchen the night before. Here I would sit in the shallow soapy water, scrubbing myself clean and washing my hair. My mother would towel dry me, wrap an old dressing gown of hers around my skinny frame and seat me in front of the range. Taking up her silver-backed hairbrush she would run its bristles through my dark brown hair until it shone. The next morning my best outfit would come out, and my father would polish my shoes while my mother supervised my dressing. My hair would be swept back and held in place with a black velvet band. Looking in the mirror I saw a different reflection to the one my peers saw at the village school. Gone was the unkempt child in crumpled clothes; in her place stood a child who looked cared for, a child who was neatly dressed, a child with loving parents.

This was the start of the second game, a game all three of us took part in, the game of happy families. It was a game directed by my mother, a game of acting out her dream, the dream of a happy marriage, a handsome husband, a thatched house and one pretty daughter.

On our 'family' visits my mother would sit with an expression that I had already come to recognize. It was an expression that showed she was there on sufferance. A polite, slightly patronizing smile would hover on her lips, a smile which showed toleration of those visits but never enjoyment, a smile I knew would disappear immediately the visit ended and our car turned out of my grandparents' road.

Then a steady trickle of condescension would float in the air until, drop by drop, it fell into my ears. Each relative received my mother's verbal appraisal, accompanied by a laugh with no humour. I would watch the back of my father's neck growing redder as mile by mile she reminded him of his origins and, in comparison, her own worth.

If my mother's memory of my father remained locked on the handsome 'Paddy' who had danced her off her feet, in his eyes she remained for ever the classy English woman who was too good for him.

As my mother regurgitated her views of the day, my pleasure would evaporate until, by the time my bedroom was reached, it was a distant memory. The game of happy families had ended and I knew it would not be played again until the next visit.

Just before our last Christmas at the thatched house we visited my grandparents again. To my delight, in the tiny back room where my grandfather had at one time mended shoes, was a strange-looking bird. It was bigger than a chicken, with grey plumage and a red gullet. A chain attached to one of its legs, secured it to a ring in the wall. It looked at me with what I saw as hope. Hope for company. Hope for freedom. On asking my grandparents what it was called they simply said 'a turkey'.

I promptly christened him Mr Turkey. At first, mindful of his beak, which was considerably bigger than a chicken's, I simply sat and chattered to him. Later, seeing how docile he was, I grew braver and reached out my hand to stroke him. The bird, disorientated by his surroundings, allowed me to pet him without protest and I believed I had made another feathered friend. No one told me what the fate of my new friend was going to be.

My grandparents had invited us for Christmas Day, and I dutifully wore the uniform and played the role of the child of a happy family. A small Christmas tree, overburdened with red and gold decorations, stood in the window of the small cramped sitting room. Chattering relatives occupied every available space, while plentiful drinks were poured, passed round and consumed. My father, flushed with alcohol, was the centre of attention. He was the joking, jovial, favourite son and adored brother in his family, and I was loved because I was his.

My grandparents had moved their small table from its place by the window, where the tree now stood, to the centre of the room. The table's extensions were so seldom used that they seemed to be of a lighter wood, once it was extended to accommodate eight people. Cutlery had been polished, Christmas crackers arranged beside each setting and borrowed chairs had been placed around it. I was seated opposite my father.

Delicious smells wafted from the tiny kitchen along with the noise of great activity. Meat, boiled vegetables, crispy roast potatoes all swimming in gravy were put onto plates and carried to the table by my grandmother and aunt. My mother had not offered to help, nor was she asked to.

As I looked at my piled-high plate of food, my mouth watered; breakfast had been a hurried weak cup of tea and a digestive biscuit. Impatiently, I waited for the first adult to commence so that I could follow, and then my father pointed to the meat and told me what had happened to my friend.

Nausea replaced hunger, silence hung in the air for a few seconds as I looked around the table in disbelief. My father's eyes both mocked and challenged me. I saw the amusement in the adult faces as they exchanged glances and I forced myself to show no feeling. Instinctively I knew that if I refused to eat, not only would he be pleased, but somehow in that mysterious adult world where children's feelings are not real, any tears shed for Mr Turkey would be gently mocked.

I ate it, even though every mouthful stuck in my throat. As I forced it down a hopeless rage rose inside me; hatred was born that Christmas. Laughter around the table became the sound of adults conspiring and my childhood, although still not completely gone, only hung on by a few threads.

Crackers were pulled, hats were placed on top of heads and faces grew flushed, both from the heat of the fire and the whiskey diluted with water that everyone, except my mother and I, drank in copious quantities. She had her bottle of dry sherry while I drank orange squash.

My mind stayed on the big gentle bird that had looked so forlorn when he had lived in that tiny back room for the last days of his life. I felt shame that Christmas had meant he had to die and shame that to protect myself from ridicule I had swallowed that meat.

The Christmas pudding was served next and my portion had the silver coin. Then it was time to open our presents. My grandparents gave me a new jumper, my aunt and uncles hair ribbons, slides, trinkets and a doll. My parents handed me a large parcel with an English postmark. Once opened it revealed several Enid Blyton books with my name written in them from my English grandmother. I was filled with a feeling of such longing to see her again as memories flooded in of my earlier, happier days. I saw again her small, neatly dressed figure, heard her voice calling 'Antoinette, where are you?', heard my own laughter as I pretended to hide and smelt her perfume of lilies and face powder as she bent down to kiss me. Somehow, I thought, if she was there our home would be happy again.

My parents gave me a pencil case for school and two second-hand books. Fairly soon after that it was time to go.

That night we drove back to the thatched house and I went straight to bed, too tired to hear the scurrying in the thatch, or to switch on the torch.

On Boxing Day I went for a walk on my own, for once leaving the dogs behind in the hope of seeing rabbits and hares playing. There was a field at the top of a slight hill where I could lie to watch them. That morning I was to be disappointed. The weather was too cold for me and for them.

It was not until Easter that my patience was rewarded as I lay motionless on top of the daisy-spotted hillock. I held my breath, scared that the slightest noise would alert the rabbit families. I stayed out of sight, but close enough to see the whites of their bobtails. Whole families left their burrows to gambol in the field below and welcome the spring in. That day I came across a baby rabbit that seemed to have been abandoned by its parents. It sat, unmoving, with its bright eyes flickering nervously as I bent to pick it up. Tucking it under my jumper for warmth I could feel its heart beating rapidly as I raced home.

'What have you got there?' exclaimed my mother, seeing the bulge of the rabbit.

Pulling my jumper up I showed her and she gently took it from me.

'We'll make a home for it until it's big enough to find its family,' she said.

Gathering newspapers, she showed me how to shred them so that they would provide a warm nest, then she found a wooden box and the first of the makeshift cages was made. When the farmers found that we had one rescued rabbit they brought us several more. They explained that dogs and foxes often killed the parents, leaving the young unable to fend for themselves. The care of these orphaned rabbits was something my mother and I did together. We put straw, water and food into the cages and fed them by hand.

'When they're big,' she warned me, 'you can't keep them as pets any more. These are wild rabbits. They belong in the fields. But we'll keep them until they're strong enough to be released.'

My father silently watched my mother and I doing this together. Always sensitive to his moods, I felt his growing resentment, aware of his gaze. For once he said nothing, as it was an interest my mother shared with me.

A few weeks after the first rabbit had been rescued and we were preparing to release it into the fields I came downstairs to find my mother glaring at me, her face white with anger.

Before I could duck her hand rose and struck me full in the face. Her hands, surprisingly strong for someone of her size, took my shoulders and shook them. My father was watching us furtively as he warmed himself by the range with a complacent smirk on his face.

'What have I done?' were the only words that I could manage to stutter as my hair flew into my eyes and my head bounced on my neck.

'You've been in to the rabbits. You left the door open. The dogs got in. They've torn them to pieces.'

'I shut the door last night,' I tried to protest. 'I've not been down since.'

Again her hand rose. This time she told me the slap was for my deceit. Then she dragged me into the back room to show me the carnage. Bits of tail were on the bloodstained floor, clumps of fur were scattered everywhere and the only parts left whole were the paws. I wanted to scream but my throat seemed to close as my body shook with suppressed sobs.

On her instructions I filled a pail with water and started to scrub the blood from the floor. As I worked the one thought that filled my head was that I knew I had shut the cage door.

Chapter Eight

Life at the thatched house continued, each day blending into the next: the walks to school, my weekend tasks and 'the drives'. Occasionally the routine would be broken by a visit to my grandparents, but the joy of visiting them had diminished since Christmas.

One Saturday, when I collected the milk from the nearby farm, the farmer's wife invited us all for high tea on the following Sunday. She gave me a note to give to my mother and to my delight my parents accepted.

High tea in the country was served at six o'clock, as the farming community rose at dawn and retired early in the evening. The game of happy families started as soon as I, freshly bathed with neatly brushed hair, was dressed in my best outfit. I had been hoping to explore the farm, so I was reluctant to put it on, knowing my mother, fearful of it getting dirty, never liked me to play in it.

On our arrival, as though reading my mind, the farmer's

wife said to her two sons, 'Take Antoinette out and show her around the farm. She likes animals.'

I rushed eagerly outside with the two boys before my mother could warn me about keeping clean. Even though they were a couple of years older than me they'd always seemed shy but once outside, away from the adults, they became friendly. Firstly they showed me a sty with a fat sow lying motionless on her side, each teat covered by greedily guzzling piglets, she seemingly oblivious to them. On hearing our voices she opened one white-lashed eye; seeing we were no threat to her young, she sleepily shut it and resumed her slumber. Next I followed the boys to where the cows were being electronically milked. The large bovine creatures paid us no attention as they stood patiently while the machinery drained their udders. Nearby was an outhouse where butter was still made with a hand-turned churn. Finally we entered a barn where the hay had been made into bales and stacked up to roof height. A ladder rested against the tallest pile and, squealing with laughter, we played a type of hide and seek until the farmer's wife called us in.

The boys had to go and wash, because they had been helping their father on the farm that day, even though it was a Sunday. The farmer came in to get ready for tea, and my mother offered to help his wife lay the table.

'Antoinette, when you went out, did you see the kittens?' the farmer's wife asked.

'No,' I replied.

My father was the nice father that day and took me by the

hand. 'Come on,' he said. 'While they're getting tea ready I'll take you there, we'll look for them together.'

It was the last day I believed in the nice father.

Still holding my hand, he led me to the barn where just a few minutes earlier the boys and I had been playing. Going to the back we found the nest of multi-coloured kittens, ranging from jet black to a marmalade gold, so young their eyes were still a milky blue. As I looked at them one yawned, showing dainty white teeth. Between them protruded a small, very pink tongue. Lulled by the intoxicating farm aromas and enchanted by the wriggling bundles of fluff, I knelt down to stroke their silky fur. I looked up at my father longingly, hoping that maybe he would let me have one. As my eyes met his I froze: the nice father had disappeared; I saw the gleam in his eyes, saw his mocking gaze and felt again that lump of fear that controlled my voice box, rendering me speechless.

As though in slow motion I felt his hands roughly lift my frock, felt the yank on my knickers as they were pulled down to my ankles, felt the roughness of the straw on my bare body, felt him penetrate me and felt his shudders a few seconds later. Slime trickled down my leg but when I looked down all I could see were my freshly polished black shoes with my white knickers draped on them.

As he buttoned up his flies he took a clean handkerchief from his pocket and threw it at me. As though through a tunnel, I heard his voice say, 'Clean yourself up with that, my girl.'

The happiness I had felt that day dissolved, the sun disappeared and in its place twilight coloured the world, turning it into a grey unfriendly place. I did as he'd told me, while he watched.

'Ready, Antoinette?' he asked as he brushed me down. Then, putting on his 'nice father's' face, he took my hand and led me back to the house for tea.

The farmer's wife was all smiles. Thinking my downcast face was because my father had not let me keep a kitten, she said: 'They don't make good pets, Antoinette. Farm cats are only interested in catching rats.'

I looked at her mutely. Speech eluded me and numbly I took my place at the table. We sat down for a generous Irish high tea. She had laid out a spread of home-cured ham, roasted chicken, hard-boiled eggs, salad, potato cakes, soda bread and homemade jam. She kept saying: 'Antoinette, come on, eat.' Then she remarked to my mother: 'She's very quiet today.'

My mother's eyes caught mine with a look of disdain that froze me, and then she turned to the farmer's wife with her polite smile fixed firmly in place and answered, 'She's such a bookworm, my daughter. She's not a great chatterer.'

Other than visiting my grandparents, I can remember no other family days out during that period of my life.

As I sat in the hospice lounge, I thought about that little girl who had once been me. I thought about her when she was a trusting toddler, trusting in the love of her mother, and having no reason to doubt other adults. I saw again the picture of her smiling confidently into the camera when she was three. I thought of her excitement at travelling to Northern Ireland, her joy at starting a new school, her love of her dog. I wondered then what Antoinette would have been like had she been allowed to grow up normally.

I felt her presence as another picture was forced into my mind. I saw a dark room; in it a small, frightened child was hunched tightly up in bed, a thumb in her mouth for comfort. Her dark brown curls were plastered damply on the back of her neck while her eyes were wide open. She was too scared to close them in case her nightmare returned: the nightmare of being chased, of being out of control; the nightmare that still haunted my sleep began with her then.

Knowing that the days of calling out to her mother had gone, she could only lie and shiver until sleep returned to force her eyes unwillingly shut.

Then I remembered for the first time in many years the ultimate betrayal of that little girl, the betrayal that sealed her fate. Only by hiding her in the depths of my memory and creating Toni could there have been survival.

If I could have reached my arms out to her through the decades, I would have picked her up and taken her somewhere safe, but Antoinette was no longer there to be saved.

I kept coming back to the same question: 'Why did my mother go into such a state of denial that enabled such a childhood?'

I'd always thought of my mother as having had a ruined life, never having any happiness, her life destroyed by my father's selfishness. I'd always seen that she came from a comfortable English middle-class background, had never been happy in Northern Ireland and believed she had simply married the wrong man. But there, for the first time, with no diversions to take my mind away from these memories, it dawned on me exactly what my mother had done. She knew when I told her of that kiss what would inevitably follow. She was thirty-six years old when I told her, a woman who had gone through a war. She took me away from the school where I was happy. A school which had some of the most qualified teachers in Northern Ireland, and where the headmistress, a diligent and intelligent woman, would have recognized the change in a child and questioned the reasons why. That was when my mother, I realized, became my father's accomplice.

'Now do you understand, Toni?' came the whisper. 'Now do you understand what she did?'

'No,' I replied. 'No, I don't understand what she did. I want her to tell me. I want her to tell me why.'

'Remember the games, Toni,' came the whisper.

First there was his game of 'our secret'. Then there was the game of 'happy families', and her final game of Ruth, 'the victim'.

My mind went back to the many occasions that she used her English accent and lady-like demeanour to talk herself out of situations, convincing people I was the difficult child and she was the long-suffering mother of one.

She knew that with a four-mile walk home from school there'd be no time for me to have friends. The children who attended the village school all lived near to it, so during the weekends and holidays I would be isolated. There was nobody I was going to confide my troubles to.

I suppose, I thought sadly, that was something I'd always known. I had never stopped loving my mother, for that is something children do. I was never able to stop, never had the desire to stop. But I wondered now, when she only had such a short time to live, if finally she would offer me some explanation. Would she finally admit that she had not been a victim, that the guilt she'd tried to make me feel was not my guilt? Would some plea for forgiveness come from her lips?

That's what I wanted, that's what I hoped for, as I returned to my mother's bedside and drifted into sleep in the reclining chair.

Chapter Nine

A black fog of depression hung over the thatched house. It swirled around our heads, pervading our minds. It poisoned the atmosphere and became words; words which acted as tools of bitterness, reproach and anger. Hers were always the same recriminations. He gambled, he drank, he'd lost his severance pay. Her voice chased him from the house, following him to the gate. The force of his anger would float back, lingering like a black shadow in every corner of the house.

Tea chests again stood in the living room and the dogs, as though sensing a question mark over their future, hid under the table.

My mother had already told me that we would have to move. Upstairs, when I'd gone to bed, I would pull the bedclothes over my head to block out the anxiety, which the constant sound of their anger bred.

The isolation of the poultry farm, the cold and the lack of

money, for however hard she worked there was never enough, stoked her fury. But one smile from my father could always dispel it.

My mother's ambition had always been to be a house owner, as her family had been before her. Here her hopes of a profitable business had folded; it was a struggle to pay the rent, and there was certainly nothing left over to save.

'Antoinette,' she informed me one evening, 'tomorrow I'm going to take you to meet an old lady. If she likes you, we might be going to live with her. I want you to be on your best behaviour and if we move there you'll go back to your old school. You'd like that, wouldn't you?'

I could feel the hope rise up in me but I tried to conceal it as I replied: 'Yes, Mummy, I would like that very much.'

That night I went to bed clinging to that nugget of hope. Could I really leave that village school where I was so disliked and go back to a school where I'd been popular? Then other thoughts came into my head: who was this old lady and why was my mother taking me and not my father? Questions that I could not find the answers to buzzed around my head until I fell into a fitful sleep.

I awoke early the next morning and the memory of the previous night's conversation with my mother jumped straight to the forefront of my mind. A feeling of excitement coursed through my body, a feeling that I tried to suppress because I didn't want it to be followed by disappointment.

Was I really going to have a day out with my mother, and might I be going back to my old school, leaving behind the village school that I hated so much? Hope burned inside me as I went down the stairs.

Pans of water boiling on the stove reassured me when my mother told me they were for my wash. By the time I'd finished breakfast the tin bath was filled. Undressing quickly I immersed myself in the water. First I soaped myself all over, enjoying the feeling of the soapy water trickling through my fingers, and then I rinsed my body with my face-cloth, washed my hair in the heated rainwater and rinsed it until I could hear it squeak with cleanliness, before being briskly towel dried. Next my mother took her silver-backed hairbrush and with slow strokes commenced to brush. Lulled by the hypnotic rhythm of the brush and relaxed by the warmth of the stove, I leant against her knees, basking in the attention. A sense of security enfolded me with her ministrations. I wished they still took place every night, as once they had.

Once my mother had tied my hair back with a ribbon, she laid out my best outfit, gave me a pair of clean white socks and polished my shoes. When we were both ready my father drove us into Coleraine, where my mother and I caught a bus, which took us a few miles into the countryside.

When the bus dropped us off, we walked a few yards until we came to the entrance of a driveway that was partially obscured by overgrown hedgerows. On a tree was nailed a sign that simply read 'Cooldaragh'.

No gate barred our entry so, with me holding her hand, we walked up the long drive. The trees on either side formed a latticework as their untrimmed branches spread above our heads until, almost touching, they created a cool green lacy ceiling. At their roots long, coarse grass tangled with nettles and encroached onto the gravel. Just as I was wondering where we were going we turned a bend and I saw Cooldaragh for the first time. I gasped. It was the biggest and most beautiful house I'd ever seen.

As we approached it, two dogs ran towards us with their tails wagging, followed by a stately old lady. She was tall and thin, with white hair pinned up on top of her head. Her erect stance belied the need of the walking stick that she held in her left hand, as she offered her right one to my mother. She reminded me of characters I'd seen in sepia photographs of another era. As my mother shook her hand she introduced us.

'This is my daughter, Antoinette,' she said with her hand on my shoulder and a smile on her face. 'And this, Antoinette, is Mrs Giveen.'

Shyness overcame me and silenced my tongue, but, seeming to understand that, the old lady smiled at me.

Mrs Giveen led us inside to a room where a tea tray was already laid. Even I, young as I was, soon realized that this was a type of interview and that I, as well as my mother, was being assessed and judged. She asked me several questions, such as what I liked doing and what my hobbies were. Then she started asking me about my school and whether I liked it.

Before I could answer, my mother jumped in. 'She did very well when she went to her junior school in town. But unfortunately we had to move. Then it was just too far for us to send her. But she certainly liked it there, didn't you, Antoinette?'

I confirmed that I did.

My mother continued. 'If we moved here, there's a bus that could take her to school every day. One of the reasons I would like to make this move is so that my daughter could go back to the school where she was so happy.'

The old lady looked at me and asked, 'Antoinette, is that what you would like to do?'

I felt my heart move to my throat. 'Oh, yes. I would like to go back to my old school very much.'

After tea she suddenly held her hand out to me. 'Come, child. Let me show you around.'

Although she didn't remind me of either of my grandmothers, having neither their warmth nor affectionate natures, I instinctively liked her. She talked to me as she led me outside and introduced me to her dogs, whom she obviously loved. She placed her hand on the terrier, whose colouring reminded me of Judy.

'This one has been with me since he was a puppy. He's thirteen years old now and is called Scamp.'

She patted the larger dog, who gazed at her adoringly.

'And this is Bruno. He's a cross between an Alsatian and a Collie. He's two now.'

She asked me about my dogs. I told her about Judy, how I got her for my fifth birthday, how I'd rescued Sally and brought her home. I even told her about June, the bantam. She reassured me as she patted me on the shoulder.

'If you come here, you can bring your dogs. There's plenty of space for them.'

I sighed with relief. It was the one question I'd not asked which had been on my mind. As I watched her dogs playing on the lawn, I noticed large flowering bushes big enough for a child to play in, which she told me were called rhododendrons. Behind them, was woodland with tall, shady trees.

'I have my own Christmas tree plantation,' Mrs Giveen told me. 'So that at Christmas I'm always able to choose my own tree.'

I began to feel very comfortable with her. I continued chattering as she took me around to the side of the house, where small stocky ponies grazed in a large field. Trustingly, they came to the fence and gazed at us with their heavily fringed, dark, liquid eyes. As she leant over the fence to gently stroke them, Mrs Giveen explained that they were old retired ponies that had once worked carting peat from the bogs. Now they could roam free and end their lives in peace. Straightening up, she took some sugar cubes from her pocket and held them out to the little ponies. I watched with wonder as their velvet noses nuzzled her hand, gently removing the sugar cubes.

'So Antoinette,' she asked out of the blue. 'Would you like to come and live here?'

To me the house and grounds seemed to be magical, like places I'd read about in my fairy-tale books. I had never dreamt I could live in such a place. Still hardly daring to believe that she meant it, I looked up at her and simply said, 'Yes, I'd like that very much.'

She smiled at me again as she took me back to my mother, showing both of us around the house. First we went into a huge hunting hall, muskets and an assortment of crude-handled knives decorating the wall above a large marble fireplace. I was later told they had been hung there by her grandfather, who had fought the Indians in America. A thick oak door opened from the hall into her private lounge, furnished with, to my untrained eye, very elegant, delicate and spindly-legged chairs and settees. I learnt over the following months that they were valuable antiques from the Louis Quinze period.

As the two women talked, I realized that my mother was being interviewed for the position of housekeeper and companion. Mrs Giveen, it seemed, no longer had enough money to staff a house of that size since the opening of factories in Northern Ireland had brought an end to the age of cheap labour.

My father, I gathered, was to carry on with his own work as a mechanic in the town. With no rent to pay and an income coming in from her new job, my mother hoped that she could save towards buying her own home.

After I learnt we were going to live there, I could sense I had passed some test and my mother was very happy and pleased with me. I can't really remember her packing up the thatched house, but we had very few possessions and much of our old furniture was, I think, left behind. The chickens were sold to nearby farmers, including my bantam, June, which made me feel sad. We still only seemed to have a few suitcases and the now battered tea chests to our name. As on all our previous moves, my mother filled them with clothes, bedding and books.

On our arrival at Cooldaragh, Mrs Giveen met us at the door.

'Antoinette, dear,' she said, 'come with me and I will show you your room.'

She took me through the hunting hall, up the main staircase to a gallery with several doors leading off it. She showed me my large room, furnished with an old-fashioned brass bed, covered with a thick down quilt. Beside it was a cloth-covered bedside table with an oil lamp placed on it. By the window was a small desk and next to it a bookcase. Then she told me, to my delight, that her room was next to mine. That news made me feel very safe.

There were two other staircases, which led to the disused servants' quarters. One had been for the male servants and one for the females. My parents had the housekeeper's bedroom, which was near to the only bathroom in the house. In the past, when the house had a full complement of servants, the bath water had been heated on the peat-fired range in the kitchen and carried upstairs by an army of maids. Now carrying the numerous pans of water needed for our weekly baths became an onerous task.

At the base of those stairs were two more rooms, which had once been the butler's and maids' pantries. A door opened into a small courtyard, where a pump supplied our drinking water. Rain butts collected more water for all our other needs and every morning buckets had to be filled and placed beside the range.

A long, red-tiled corridor led from the kitchen and pantries back into the main body of the house, where my parents' sitting room was positioned.

Later, when I explored the house on my own, I counted twenty-four rooms. Only four bedrooms were furnished, two of which myself and my parents occupied. The smallest and dustiest rooms, which had no furniture, were the now unused servants' quarters.

Not only was there neither running water nor electricity at Cooldaragh, with the whole house lit by oil lamps or candles, but the bus also only went into town once a day, leaving in the morning and returning after six in the evening. It was arranged that I would be a day boarder at school. That meant I could stay in the warm library to do my homework and have my supper with the full-time boarders, while I waited for the bus.

Once we had settled in, my mother had to take me shopping for a new uniform to go back to Coleraine High School. Even though I'd been pleased at the thought of returning, I was no longer the happy, confident child they had previously known, having become much more withdrawn. Because time had elapsed and the teachers had not seen the gradual change in me, they seemed to put it down to the difference that time had made.

My father was absent most weekends, 'working overtime' as my mother always explained, which was relief for me. On those days she and I would have lunch with Mrs Giveen in her dining room. Like her drawing room it was furnished with antiques, the surface of the mahogany sideboard completely covered in silverware. We three sat at the glowingly polished table, which was big enough to accommodate ten people. My mother, who was never a wonderful cook, could manage a roast at the weekend. Looking back, I would say my father deliberately stayed away, because Mrs Giveen was one of a dying breed, the aristocracy of Northern Ireland. My father always felt intimidated by such people, whereas my mother was comfortable in their company. I think in her mind she could pretend to herself that she was a friend as opposed to the housekeeper.

The old lady was in her eighties and exuded a sense of pride and dignity. I intuitively knew she was lonely, and we shared a bond that so often exists between the very young and the old. After lunch, I would help my mother clear away and wash up at the deep white sink in the maids' pantry. Then I would go out into the grounds with all the dogs. I would play in the rhododendron bushes, which were tall enough to stand upright in, or visit the diminutive shaggy ponies. If I gave them titbits they would let me fondle their soft noses and stroke their necks.

I felt safe in those days, because of where I was sleeping. My father didn't dare come near me, with Mrs Giveen's bedroom just the other side of the wall.

On rainy days I explored the house. Mrs Giveen had cupboards full of mementos from the American wars and would enjoy talking about her grandfather and showing me all his souvenirs.

On other days I would take a book into the vast kitchen, which was always filled with delicious baking smells from the various breads and cakes my mother made. Here all the cooking was done on the old peat-fuelled range. Before I lost myself in adventures with the Famous Five or went swimming with the famous Water Babies, I would be given various tasks to do. I would be sent outside to bring in pails of drinking water from the pump. I collected peat for the range and baskets of logs for the fires in our rooms. On fine days, which in the Northern Irish winter were not too frequent, I would walk in the woods, collecting fallen branches and sturdy twigs for fires. These we would place at the back of the stove to dry, then use as kindling. My mother had read somewhere that tea made from stinging nettles had medicinal qualities, so, armed with gardening gloves, I filled baskets with the green weeds, which she then simmered on the range, filling the kitchen with a pungent aroma.

On the winter school mornings, when I made my candle-lit way along corridors to fetch water for washing, I could hear the scurrying of mice. I wasn't frightened of them, simply looking on them as an inconvenience because their presence meant every scrap of food had to be placed into tins or jars. One morning I saw that my father had left a packet of sugar out when he had returned home late. Sitting in it was a plump mouse with small beady eyes and twitching whiskers. I chased it away and threw out the remaining sugar. Even though Cooldaragh had an army of cats, every morning fresh mouse droppings appeared and my job was to clean them up.

Easter came and went, bringing with it improved weather. Then I was able to return to spending most of my time exploring the woods with the dogs. I would walk through the leaf-carpeted woodland, warmed by the rays of the sun that shone on the new green foliage. I heard the joyful notes of birdsong as egg-filled nests were guarded by the future parents. Scamp, who had become blind, was too old now for those walks, but the other three happily accompanied me, racing around beside me, digging in the undergrowth. Judy would often desert me in a hopeful hunt for rabbits. Bruno, on my command of, 'Go fetch', would search for her and herd her back.

Between the Christmas tree plantation and the woodland ran a stream. There I'd lie, looking for frogspawn, tickling the water with a stick to see if any life lurked in the mud. My patience would often be rewarded by the sight of small frogs that had only just left their tadpole stage behind, or a glimpse of the toads that lurked in the primrose-dotted clumps of grass.

In the early evenings, I would walk with Mrs Giveen to give the ponies titbits. They always knew the time we were coming, standing up against the fence, patiently waiting for us. On returning to the house I would help my mother prepare the high tea that had to be ready before my father was due back from work. I would take Mrs Giveen's tray to her lounge then return to the kitchen to eat with my parents.

My father said very little to me in those months. I could sense, still, his eyes following me, but on the whole he ignored me, and I him.

Those days were a peaceful interlude in my life, an interlude that as time went by I assumed would last for ever, but how could it?

At the beginning of my school summer holidays, I woke up to an eerie silence in the house. I could sense something was wrong as I went down the back stairs to the kitchen. As my mother made my breakfast, she told me that Mrs Giveen had died peacefully in the night. She spoke to me very gently, knowing how fond I was of the old lady. A feeling of desolation crept over me for I knew that she had inadvertently been my protector as well as my friend. I wanted to say goodbye to her; I went up the stairs into her bedroom, where she lay on her bed with her eyes closed and a bandage tied around her chin to the top of her head. I wasn't scared the first time I saw death. I just knew she was no longer there.

The dogs were quiet that day. They seemed to feel as I did, that we had lost a friend. That evening I gave the ponies their titbits, stroked their necks and found some comfort in their solemn gaze.

I don't remember the funeral or relatives coming, but obviously they happened. What I do remember is her daughter-in-law coming to stay for a few weeks, mainly to do an inventory of the house, especially of all the antiques. She was a charming, lovely woman, who always smelled of perfume. She would invite me into her room, which was on the other side of mine, and give me gifts of hair slides and ribbons. Most excitingly, she brought me a tartan dress from London. My mother, an experienced dressmaker, made me my first suit out of grey flannel. I was very proud of my suddenly grown-up appearance, which I saw reflected in the mirror, and looked forward to wearing it when young Mrs Giveen took me to church.

It was during her visit that the Sunday service was interrupted by the appearance of a small bat, which suddenly appeared and swooped over our heads. To me it was just a flying mouse; to the panicked congregation it was a creature that instilled fear. That Sunday the service was cut short. Grown-ups, I decided, were scared of the most peculiar things.

It was the first time I had really seen my mother with another woman of comparable age, whose company she enjoyed. Instinctively, I had always known she did not enjoy my paternal grandmother's or my aunt's company. Often at weekends the three of us would sit in the garden at the side of the house, where we would have afternoon tea in the English fashion. My mother would wheel out a tea trolley with daintily cut sandwiches of egg and cress, or thinly sliced, home-cooked ham. There would be freshly baked scones with jam and cream, followed by fruit cake, all washed down by tea, poured from a silver teapot into china cups. My mother and young Mrs Giveen would talk and on those days I felt very grown up because I was included in the conversations.

The day I was dreading arrived, the day that Mrs Giveen junior told me she had to return to her house in London. Before she went she gave me a present.

'Antoinette,' she said, 'I know it's soon to be your birthday. I'm sorry I won't be here for it, but I have got you a little present.'

She gave me a small gold locket on a chain, which she hung around my neck.

Now, with the house empty, my mother, I think, felt she was mistress. Which indeed, for the next year, she was.

Chapter Ten

The golden glow of sunbeams brushed my eyelids, forcing them apart. Sleepily, my eyes flickered around the room. The rays of sun settled on my new tartan dress hanging on the back of the door, intensifying the reds and blues of the plaid, turning them into jewel-like colours.

A twinge of excitement told me that this was my tenth birthday. This was the day I was to have my first party; every girl in my class was expected, all fourteen of them. My father, on hearing that my mother had agreed with this, had informed us he was going to spend the day playing golf, thus giving me a special present – his absence. This was my day and the first half of it I could spend with my mother alone. His presence would not be there to cast a cloud on a day I felt was mine.

My gaze alighted on the gold locket and chain that young Mrs Giveen had given me and with a pang I wished that both she and her mother-in-law could be present. My mother had told me during the summer holidays that this year I could have a party. My thoughts drifted back to taking the invitations into school. All the girls in my class had accepted and I was excited at the prospect of showing them my home. For in my mind, as well as my mother's, Cooldaragh was my home.

The dogs and I would always end up on our walks in the Christmas tree plantation, where I thought of the young Giveens choosing their very own tree year after year, and then taking it back to the huge hall. I pictured them, dressed in the more formal clothes that I had seen in the sepia-tinted photographs hanging in the drawing room, climbing up a ladder to decorate it. I pictured them on Christmas morning in front of a log fire opening their presents, while the servants stood in the background waiting for their big day to follow.

Lying in my bed, I stretched my toes, wanting to stay for just a few more moments. This was the Cooldaragh I wanted to share with my classmates. I wanted them to feel the magic that I did.

My mother's voice, calling up the stairs, broke into my reveries. Pulling on my old clothes, which were folded on my bedside chair, I went downstairs to find her. Delicious smells of baking drifted up the corridor, informing me that she was already at work.

I knew that my cake, iced in pink with ten white candles mingled with the words 'Happy Birthday', had been baked the day before. When I entered the kitchen I saw more rows of small cakes cooling on racks. Next to them stood the coveted bowl, which I knew after breakfast I could lick out once the cooled icing, liberally dotted with the bright colours of hundreds and thousands, had been spread on the cakes.

There was the table laid for two; a teapot covered in its knitted cosy standing in the middle, brown eggs in white egg cups and, beside the plates, a small pile of parcels.

'Happy birthday darling,' my mother said as she greeted me with a kiss. This, I felt, was going to be a perfect day. Unwrapping the presents I found a pair of new shoes from my parents, shiny black with a little strap that went across the instep; a Fair Isle jumper from my Irish grandparents; and three books by Louisa M. Alcott, *Little Women*, *Little Men* and *Jo's Boys*, books I had dropped many hints that I wanted, from my English grandmother.

Tucking into my breakfast with gusto, surreptitiously passing the dogs scraps, I felt pleased it was a sunny day, happy that I had my mother to myself and delighted with my presents.

All week I had looked forward to my party. I imagined showing the girls from school around my home. Imagined them being impressed that I was lucky to live in such a place. The anticipation of being able to invite my classmates had lent more satisfaction to returning to school after the long summer holidays. Even though the holidays were enjoyable, they were also lonely. Once young Mrs Giveen had left I felt an isolation that the dogs' company could never quite dispel. Dressed in shorts, T-shirt and plimsolls I would spend my days exploring the estate with them. Taking a small bottle of squash and some sandwiches, I would sometimes disappear for most of the day, returning with dead branches and twigs, which we would use for lighting the range in the cavernous kitchen. I enjoyed my daily tasks, which now that I was a little older included sawing the dead branches from the woods into logs. But I hardly saw anyone, or left the grounds of Cooldaragh, and I missed the contact of other children. With no nearby farm, the nearest shops being in Coleraine and only the twice-daily bus service, we seldom ventured out. Instead we relied on our daily milk delivery and the twice-weekly grocery van.

However, that summer holiday had brought my mother and me closer, having to rely on one another for company. On the days it rained we would sit companionably in the kitchen, open the range door and feast on the homemade cakes she enjoyed baking. I with a book where I lost myself in the pages, and she with her knitting; the constant clicks from her needles making a soothing background noise as, with head bent, she would concentrate on the creation of each garment.

She had made me a dark green jumper, its V-neck edged in black and white, for my return to school. Other times she would place one of my woollen socks over a wooden mushroom to darn the holes that regularly appeared, or would sigh over a skirt that needed letting down until there was no hem left. Extra schoolwork always had to be done, because my school believed in setting projects for the holidays.

After breakfast was finished and I had helped my mother with the icing of the cakes, I went outside with the dogs.

My mother's warning not to venture too far, since I had to get ready for my party in good time, stopped me going to the woods. Instead I went to say good morning to the ponies. After giving them a hug and some titbits from my pocket, I headed back.

The sun was giving the red bricks of the house a warm mellow glow as I entered the courtyard, through the back door and into the kitchen. Pans of water already stood on the range, ready for me to take upstairs for my bath. It took three journeys up the steep back stairs before the water was deep enough.

I dressed in the presents from young Mrs Giveen. First the full-skirted plaid dress, with its row of buttons down the back, was pulled over my head and my mother fastened it. Then the new black shoes were slipped on over white socks, and finally my mother fastened the gold locket around my neck. My newly washed hair was brushed then tied back on the side and fastened in place with a slide. Gazing into the mirror I posed for a few seconds, liking what I saw.

Half an hour before the girls were expected I stood on the steps, my eyes firmly fixed on the drive, waiting for the first car to arrive. The dogs lay nearby, intent on keeping me company, sensing something was in the air. Like me, their gaze scanned the drive.

Within minutes of the time stated on the invitations, a convoy of black cars drove down the dusty drive. Gravel flew as they crunched to a halt in front of the steps where I waited, feeling as proprietary as my mother. Doors opened, spilling out the neatly dressed pre-teens, all clasping prettily wrapped packages. After assurances to my mother that they would all be collected at six-thirty their parents left.

My mother brought out jugs of squash as we sat on the lawn with my pile of presents. Eager faces watched me as one after another their gifts were unwrapped. Wrapping paper was removed to reveal boxes of sweets, which were laughingly passed around, until my mother, not wanting us to ruin our appetites, took them inside. Other parcels revealed hair slides and ribbons. A new pen in a case drew a breath of pleasure from me as did the one that contained a pink-covered diary, a diary that was never going to be written in because after that day I felt there was nothing to write about. But at the beginning of that afternoon, surrounded by my classmates, with the sun casting its warmth over us, I was not to know what was to come.

My mother helped me to gather up all the presents, then told me to show my friends around the house, which I needed no persuasion to do. I led them into the hall where, when pointing out all the American memorabilia, I caught a change in the atmosphere. There was a whisper, the odd mutter and a surprised laugh and suddenly I saw my beloved Cooldaragh through their eyes.

Instead of the grandeur I had so often described to them, I saw the blocked-up fireplaces, with newspaper stuffed into them to keep out the draughts, the cobwebs hanging in corners, the dusty carpeting on the stairs that led to the unfurnished bedrooms above. In the dining room I felt their eyes resting on the now grimy silver, unpolished since Mrs Giveen's death. I saw the threadbare curtains that had hung for so many years and noticed the oil lamps that stood on the sideboard, informing them that this huge relic of another era had no electricity.

'Where,' I heard one whisper, 'would any hot water come from?'

My classmates were products of detached houses with landscaped gardens, modern furniture and shining silver. They came from homes where their 'dailies' firmly exorcized any traces of dust and daily baths were taken for granted. They could not see the magic that I could. They could only see a derelict building. With that unerring instinct that children have, they added to the information already gleaned from their parents. They knew my mother was the caretaker. They knew I was not the product of a professional family and I was set apart from them.

I felt again that distance between us and knew I was an outsider. Curiosity not friendship was the emotion that had brought them there that day. The friendship that I had wanted to believe in was going to elude me. I felt I had stepped behind a sheet of glass. Watching through a window as my peers laughed and talked, I could only mimic them with chatter and copy their giggles. I was on the outside, looking in on someone else's party and watching myself.

That afternoon we played games, with so many rooms hide and seek was the favourite, but when it was my turn to hide somehow I knew that their search was not as diligent as when looking for one of their friends. I could feel their togetherness as they waited for the cars that would release them and return them to their sterile homes.

My mother's spread of sandwiches, fruit jellies and small iced cakes was eagerly received and washed down by more squash. The birthday cake was carried in and before it was cut I was told to blow out all the candles; if that was achieved in one go I could make a wish. Breathing as much air into my lungs as I could hold, with tightly squeezed eyes, I blew. I heard the applause and opened them. All of the candles were out and shutting my eyes firmly again I made my wish.

'Make them like me, make them my friends,' I asked, and when my eyes opened for a while I thought my wish had been granted. Now, I thought, would be a good time to pass around the sweets that had been given to me. Going to where my presents were piled up I found, to my dismay, they were all gone. They must have been eaten during our games of hide and seek when, crouched in one of the dusty unused rooms, I had waited so long to be found. Not knowing what to say I looked at my mother.

She laughed. 'Darling, you have to learn to share.'

I saw her exchange conspiratorial smiles with the girls and knew both she and they were laughing at me. I looked at the smiling faces surrounding me and my feelings of apartness returned.

As the party drew to a close I stood on the steps of Cooldaragh watching my 'friends' leaving in a convoy of cars, after politely thanking me for the day and giving vague promises of invites to their homes. Wanting to believe them, I did and waved happily at the departing cars until the last one had disappeared from sight.

Seven o'clock brought with it my father. A father whose flushed face told me he had been drinking. His stare was fixed on me. I wanted to leave, to escape it, but as always his eyes kept me firmly rooted to my seat.

My mother, in a voice pitched higher than usual, a sign which betrayed her nervousness, instructed me to show him my presents.

'Look, Paddy, what she was given.'

One by one I showed them to him.

'What no sweets?' Seeing the answer in my face he snorted. 'Did you not think to save your old man any then?'

I searched his face, was this the jovial father who could be cajoled, or the other one? I wondered, a knot of dread growing in my stomach.

The last present I showed him was my pen, black with a silver clip. As I held it out for his inspection I felt a tremor in my hand and knew by his smile he had seen it too.

'Where's your other pen, the one your mother and I bought you?' he asked and with a sinking heart I saw that he was not the jovial father that night.

'In my satchel,' was all I could stutter.

He emitted an unpleasant laugh. 'Well, get it then – sure you won't be needing two.'

'I do,' I protested. 'I need a spare, that's why Marie gave me this one.'

In front of my eyes, like the toads I had seen in the woods, he seemed to swell. His chest seemed to puff up, his eyes went bloodshot. I saw that tell-tale quiver of his mouth and too late I knew I should not have disagreed with him.

'Don't you be arguing with me, my girl,' he roared as his hand grabbed the neck of my dress and pulled me off the chair. The ground came up to meet me, the breath left my body, his hands were round my throat and dimly I heard my mother scream.

'Paddy, stop, you'll kill her!'

My hands were scrabbling with his, trying to release the fingers that gripped me as my breath wheezed and my legs flailed helplessly on the floor.

I heard him bellow, 'You do as I tell you, my girl.' Then, through the sound of my mother's pleas, I felt his grip lessen on me.

I pulled myself up, dazed and disorientated.

'Get her out of my sight,' he yelled at my mother. 'Get her to her room.'

She, without a word, took my arm and propelled me into the corridor and up the stairs, then abruptly released me. Glaring, she ordered me to stay there.

'Why do you always have to annoy him? You know he has a temper.' She sounded weary. 'Can you not try and keep the peace for my sake?' I heard a note of pleading in her voice and knew she was as afraid as I was.

Later she returned to my bedroom where, still dazed, I was trying to calm myself by escaping into *Little Women.*

Our eyes met and I knew that the protection I had felt when the Giveens were present had gone. She, I knew, had chosen to humour my father and I was relegated to being a child who was a nuisance.

'Try not to make your father angry again, Antoinette,' were her only words as she removed the oil lamp from my room and departed. I closed my eyes. As I was now unable to read, my mind invented a story. A story where I was once again loved, surrounded by friends and invited to many parties.

Back in the hospice I made myself some coffee and lit a cigarette as I tried to stop the flood of memories, but Antoinette, the ghost of my childhood, was still there. I heard her again.

'Toni, remember on your own, remember the truth.'

I had believed my past had been dealt with, but Antoinette's face kept coming back to haunt me. I had destroyed nearly all the photographs many years before, photographs that showed the life of the child who once was me, but now one by one they flashed before me.

I saw her as the chubby curly-haired toddler with shining eyes, smiling confidently into the camera, sitting crossed legged with her plump little hands holding one knee. In that photograph she was dressed in her favourite dress, smocked by her mother.

A few years later, she was wearing a checked dress, too short for her skinny frame, no socks and second-hand sandals. Her empty eyes had dark shadows under them as she looked at me. She stood on the lawns at Cooldaragh holding Judy, with her other friends, the dogs, at her feet.

In another photograph she was by the rhododendrons of Cooldaragh with the mother she loved so much. There were no photographs of her with other children or playmates.

I forced the mental pictures away and went back to my mother's bedside. As I closed my eyes I found myself looking back through the years and I remembered the unhappy, isolated child who had lived at Cooldaragh. A child whose birthday was marred, not only by the brutality of her father, and her mother's indifference to her plight, but also by her inability to interact and relate to her peers. How she watched them as though through a window, playing, laughing and chattering. She was only imitating them when she tried to join in.

It was too late for her to feel at one with them, her childhood had already gone. By her tenth birthday she knew that any happiness she felt was only a momentary illusion.

Sitting by my mother's bedside, I remembered one act of sly rebellion and it brought a wry smile to my face. It happened just after my birthday and showed that the little girl could still feel anger and that she was not a complete puppet.

At Cooldaragh all the unused fireplaces were blocked by newspaper, not only to keep some of the cold out, but also to stop birds and bats getting in. When I fetched water at dusk, I had often seen the bats swooping around the outside of the house, exploring their unseen world as darkness fell.

Watching them, I remembered that day at the church when the ringing of the church bell had disturbed one of them. I had seen the fear that its blind flight had instilled into the female section of the congregation.

I chose my night carefully, knowing that when my father took his car into Coleraine on a Friday morning, he always returned home late and drunk. I knew my mother's routine on those occasions. When she finally gave up waiting for him, she would walk down the long dark corridor that led from our sitting room to the kitchen, holding a candle to light her way. Here she would make a pot of tea, before she climbed the servants' staircase to her bedroom.

That night, knowing my mother would have thought I was asleep, I rose from my bed stealthily, determined that the bats would have maximum access to the house. I poked holes into the newspaper stuffing above the fireplaces. After that was done, I opened the back door, to where only the small courtyard separated the house from the disused stables where the bats were.

Patiently I crouched at the top of the servants' stairs, awaiting my nocturnal visitors, the instruments of my minor revenge. I was rewarded. One brave flying mouse, swooping low, entered by the back door. Once I was sure it was far enough into the house, I crept down the stairs on my bare feet and closed the door quietly.

Shivering with cold, I returned to my post on the stairs to await the results. I did not have to wait long.

I saw an orange glow as the door of my parents' sitting room opened. Then came the flicker of the candle's flame as it lit the way for my mother. I heard her scream as the bat, with its radar senses, swooped around her head.

I knew she was frozen with fear in that semi-darkness. Quickly I came down the stairs, put my arms around her, took the candle from her shaking fingers and led her back to their sitting room where I helped her into a chair. I told her I had been in the bathroom when I heard her scream.

As she sat with tears streaming down her face, I took her candle, went down to the kitchen, where the sleeping dogs hardly stirred, and made her tea. Placing a cup, milk jug and sugar on a tray where I had carefully balanced the candle, I led her up the main staircase to her bedroom, thus avoiding the bat. I placed the tray by her bedside and hugged her, because I still loved my mother.

Through my adult eyes, I tried to understand what my mother's life must have been like during those years. I could understand why she wanted to escape into her fantasy world of 'happy families', where there was nothing wrong with our lives. After all, what else did she have? After Mrs Giveen's death she had virtually no contact with other people. She had no friends or family in Northern Ireland and certainly no financial independence. Without transport, her isolation must have grown because I could sense the depression that was falling over her.

A woman of today would have choices that my mother was denied, but if she had been given them, would she have accepted a different route? What happened in later years made me doubt this.

I continued to sit by her bedside, the night-light casting a faint glow over her. I looked at her small, helpless form and saw that sleep had smoothed out some of the lines caused by pain. I felt the same conflicting emotions that the little girl had felt as she held her mother that night: bewilderment, anger and a strong desire to comfort and protect her.

Chapter Eleven

Now that the Giveens had all left, my father started coming to my bedroom again. On the days that he knew he was going to come home late, he would take his car into the town. When he returned, my mother and I would be asleep at opposite ends of the house. My room was dark, the only light coming from the moon that seemed, on fine nights, to be floating outside my window. I would often drift off to sleep, trying to see the friendly and reassuring face of the man in the moon. I had, a long time ago, lost my torch, so now that my mother had taken my lamp, I only had the candle that lit the way to my bedroom. Lying there in the dark with my fists clenched, I would squeeze my eyes tightly shut, hoping if I didn't open them, he wouldn't be there. But he always was. I would try and huddle deeper under the bedclothes. Then I would feel the cold on my body, as he pulled them down and my flannelette nightdress up.

He'd whisper into my ear, 'You like this, Antoinette, don't you?'

I'd say nothing.

He'd say, 'You'd like some pocket money, wouldn't you?'

He'd take half a crown out and push it into my fist. Then he'd take his trousers off. I'll remember always the smell of him. That whiskey breath, the stale smell of cigarettes and his body odour – no deodorant for him. He'd get on top of me. Now that I was a little bit older, although he was still careful, he could afford to be a little rougher. And he would push himself into me. I could feel those eyes of his boring through my closed eyelids. He'd tell me to open my eyes. I never wanted to. At that age, he hurt me. I heard him give a gasp before he rolled off me; he'd get off the bed, quickly pull on his clothes and go to my mother's bed.

I would be left holding half a crown.

As the visits to my room increased, so did the physical violence. One night I was playing in what had been Mrs Giveen's lounge. I'd gone in there to be alone, to be away from my parents. He came in with a newspaper and sat down. I had one of those little trinkets that looked like frogs, and came out of crackers. I was sitting aimlessly playing with it listening to the click-click sound it made. Then I felt his gaze on me.

'Antoinette,' he said, 'stop that, stop it now.'

I jumped with fear. The trinket flew out of my hand, making its final click. That was the only excuse he needed. He picked me up and threw me backwards onto the floor.

'You stop when I tell you to stop, my girl!' he shouted.

Often in the nights I would be woken by my usual nightmare. I would be dreaming of falling and falling into darkness. Then my father's presence blended into that nightmare as he woke me up. After he'd left, sleep did not return easily. In the morning I would be tired as I walked down to the kitchen to bring up my hot water to wash. I made sure that I always washed well between my legs on those mornings. It's very hard for me to remember what I felt, but I seem to remember I felt very little.

Now, with him coming to my room so often, I was getting regular 'pocket money' and I could buy friend-winning sweets again. Children, like animals, can sense when someone is weak, different or vulnerable. Even though these were nicely brought up children, where cruelty wasn't part of their make-up, they had an instinctive aversion to me. So in the early evenings, when I ate with the boarders, I avoided the ones who were my own age as much as possible. I tried to sit either with the younger girls, with whom I could play, or the older ones who were kind to me. Apart from the mealtimes I spent my time in the library with my homework. I knew I was not popular, and I could tell the teachers also knew it. The staff at that school were kind to me on the surface, but I could sense a detachment. At the age of ten, I had stopped expecting people to like me.

The bus journey home took about thirty minutes and I would try and finish my school homework, reading paragraphs of books that I knew I would be questioned about the following day. One night, my father got on at the next bus stop. He didn't sit next to me. He sat nearly opposite so he could look at me. He put on the smile of the nice father. But I no longer believed there was one. That evening I couldn't find my ticket. I could feel my father gazing at me and I felt sick with fear as I searched my satchel and pockets. I tried to whisper to the bus conductor.

'I can't find my ticket. Please don't tell my father.'

But the bus conductor just laughed. He knew I had a weekly ticket because he worked on the bus every day.

'It doesn't matter,' he said. 'Sure your father won't be cross with you. Look at him. He's smiling at you. Don't be a silly girl.'

Sure enough there sat my father, with those bloodshot eyes of his twinkling. Then he winked at me. I recognized that wink. The journey seemed to me to take for ever, even though it was only a few miles. It was dark that night and when I got off the bus it was cold. Once the bus disappeared into the distance he seized me, as I knew he would. He beat me. Across the bottom, across the shoulders with his other hand at the back of my neck, holding me roughly. He flung me about, shaking me. I didn't cry. Not then. I didn't scream. I'd stopped screaming out loud a long time ago. But as he walked me up to the house, I felt the tears trickling down my face. My mother must have seen the tracks they'd made. But she said nothing. I picked at my supper, too upset to want it, too scared to refuse it. I finished off the small amount of homework I had to do, then went to bed. I knew then I was not a child who tried to make her parents angry, but that I had a parent who looked for every excuse to find fault and hit me.

That night he came to my room when I was still awake. He wrenched the bedclothes off me. I could feel there was more violence in him than usual. I felt very afraid of him and started to cry in fright.

'I don't want any pocket money,' I said. 'I don't want you to do it to me.' Feeling hysteria rising in me, I continued to plead. 'Please, please don't do it. You hurt me.'

It was the first and the last time I cried when he came into my bedroom. My mother was in the hall and heard me. She called out, 'What's going on?'

My father called back to her: 'Nothing. She was having a nightmare. I just came in to see what it was. She's alright now.'

As he left he hissed in my ear, 'Don't you be telling your mother, my girl.'

She came into my room a few minutes later where I was huddled under the bedclothes.

'Antoinette, what happened?' she asked.

'Nothing,' I replied. 'I was having a nightmare.'

On that she left the room. She never asked me again.

On other nights I could hear the crunch of the gravel as his car drew up. Quaking with fear, I would lie in my bed, hearing the creak of the floorboards as his stealthy step approached my room. I would feign sleep on those nights, always hoping he would not want to wake me. But he did.

Not every time he came would he leave me half a crown,

but at least twice a week he did. After the first night of wrenching my fingers open and jamming it into my fist, he started mockingly to put it into the china jar on my dressing table that held my gold locket. He'd say to me, 'There's your pocket money, my girl.'

On the evenings when he came home early, I would curl up on the settee with the dogs at my feet and open a book. Often, when I read of children with loving and caring parents, the tears would spill from my eyes and slide down my face, giving my father the opportunity he was waiting for. He'd look up.

'What are you crying for, my girl?' he'd ask.

I would try and avoid looking into his eyes, as I muttered, 'Nothing.'

At that, he would get off his seat, catch hold of me by the scruff of the neck, shake me and then hit me, usually around the shoulders.

'Well, then,' he would say quietly, 'now you have something to cry about, don't you?'

My mother said nothing.

After that I stopped reading children's books about happy families. I started reading my mother's books. I did not tell her the reason. She never asked. The first adult books I read were called the White Oak Series. They were not unhappy books. But there were no children in them.

One day a man was waiting for me as I finished school. He introduced himself as a friend of my father's. He had obtained permission from the teacher who supervised the boarders to take me out to tea. I went to a teashop with him where he treated me to scones and cake, followed by ice cream. Favourite foods of little girls! He chatted to me about school. Gradually he drew me out to talk to him about my dogs. Then he asked me what I liked reading. I told him I was in the middle of a book called *Jalna* that came from the White Oak Series.

'You are very grown up for a little girl if you are reading books like that,' he said.

I glowed with happiness at his kindness and obvious interest, and the compliments he paid me. After we had finished eating and chatting, he walked me back to my school and told me how much he had enjoyed my company. He asked me if I would like him to take me out again. I replied that I would.

He visited me several times after that. I told the teachers that he was a friend of my father's and they always gave permission for him to take me. I looked forward to his visits. I felt he was interested in listening to me, which made me feel grown up and important. I could always order what I wanted. He seemed fascinated by my childish chatter. To me, who had so little interest shown, I felt I had a grown-up friend, until the final day that I saw him.

That day, on the way back from school, he took me to a grassy area. He told me again how much he liked my company. He told me he liked little girls, especially little girls as grown up as me. Then he stared at me, with what suddenly seemed like my father's eyes. He picked some blades of grass and ran his fingers up and down, up and down them suggestively.

'Antoinette,' he said, 'do you know what I would like you to do now?'

I knew.

'I know you would like that, wouldn't you, Antoinette?'

Like a rabbit caught in the sudden glare of headlamps, I froze.

'I know that you do it with your father,' he said. 'Tell the teacher; next time I come, I will take you home. Then we can spend the afternoon together before you catch your bus. You would like that, wouldn't you?'

I could only nod, as I'd been trained to do.

That night I told my father about his friend. With his face red with rage, he shook me.

'Don't you be doing this with anyone but me, my girl,' he hissed raising his fists.

But this time he lowered them without hitting me and left my room. I never saw my father's friend again and I never found out how he came to know about my father and me. It can only have been my father who told him. Even monsters, it seems, feel the pressure of living a lie; even they must have someone who knows and accepts the real person.

My life at Cooldaragh continued for a couple more months. Then my mother broke the news that the house had been sold and, yet again, we would have to move, this time back across the Irish Sea to Kent. She as well as my father needed to work, she explained, for now that we could no longer live rent free my father's income alone would not support us. Employment for her, she believed, would be easier to find in England.

My mother then told me that in the two years we had spent at Cooldaragh she had managed to save enough money for a deposit on a house. The harsh lines that had appeared around her mouth over the last few years seemed to soften as she talked, for finally she could see that her dream – that of owning her own home – was drawing closer.

I saw the enthusiasm on her face but I could not share it with her, as I had grown to love Cooldaragh.

Chapter Twelve

Added to my anxiety at leaving Cooldaragh was the fact that my mother had told me I was not going to live with them when we moved. Instead, I was going to be sent to stay with my godmother in Tenterden. Arrangements had already been made for me to attend the local school there. Even though she assured me that this was only a temporary arrangement, until she and my father found a house for all of us, I felt I was going to be abandoned. Family life might have been terrible, but being handed over to the care of strangers was even more frightening.

Far from being upset at the prospect of being parted from me, my mother only seemed to be tearful at having to find a home for Bruno, her favourite dog. He was to go to the South of Ireland, where Mrs Giveen's daughter lived.

To add to my grief, my parents decided that Sally, even though she was happy with us, was to be put to sleep. Patiently, my mother explained to me that the little dog had never recovered from her early life. She had started to have fits, and it would be unfair to re-home her.

Tearfully I asked about Judy and the cats. The cats were to stay at Cooldaragh, while Judy was to board with a nearby farmer until we were all settled.

I felt devastated to be leaving Cooldaragh and the only school I had been happy at. I felt my whole life had gone as I said my tearful goodbyes to the animals. The first was to Bruno, who cheerfully went off in his new mistress's car. I stood at the end of the drive watching the car disappear, hoping he would be as loved by them as he had been by me.

The second and harder goodbye was to Sally. What felt like unbearable grief nearly overwhelmed me when, thinking she was going for an outing, she trustingly jumped into my father's car. I reached through the window to stroke her for the last time, trying not to let her see the tears that threatened to choke me. I knew she was being sent on her last journey to the vet's because my father had informed me of the fact that day.

I remember the pain I felt, and wonder why a man who was such an accomplished liar had to tell the truth that day. I had to face that the truth had also come from my mother. What would one white lie to protect me have mattered then, when our whole family life was built on lies? Although my mother tried to comfort me, she couldn't make me feel any better. I felt I had sent one of my friends to her death.

Over the next few weeks I helped my mother pack the tea chests again and packed my case for my stay with my godmother, of whom I had no memory at all. Because I was only allowed one small case, some of my treasured possessions had to go, Jumbo being the first casualty.

A few days before we were due to depart all our belongings were collected to go into storage. The following day my father took Judy to the farmer. I wanted to go with her, but my fear of being alone with him outweighed my wish to accompany her. I patted and hugged her as she sat in the car, and she, sensing my unhappiness, simply licked my hand.

As I stood and watched the car disappear I felt totally alone, all my friends had left. I knew that my mother also felt sad, but this time I felt little love for her, just dull resentment.

The day came when our few personal possessions were loaded into the car and, with me squashed into the back, we drove to the Belfast ferry. This would take us to Liverpool from where, after the twelve-hour crossing, we would continue our long journey to Kent. This time after the crossing, as we arrived at Liverpool, I felt no sense of excitement, just a dead sense of depression.

The next stage, on the long drive to Kent, I tried to read, but vivid pictures kept coming into my head. Sally looking at me, with her trusting brown eyes, as she went on her last journey. I could still feel the silky hair on her head when I had stroked it. I saw the ponies as they waited for me at the fence when I had said a last goodbye to them as I fed them their titbits. The feel and smell of them as I threw my arms around their necks for the last time still lingered. I saw faithful Bruno looking out of the window as he disappeared from view, and I missed Judy unbearably.

I looked at the back of my parents' heads as we drove; my mother's often turned towards him as she talked quietly. Occasionally she would turn to me, but I kept my book up to mask the feelings that I knew would have shown, feelings of resentment at my oncoming abandonment and anger at parting with my friends.

Every few hours we would stop by the roadside for sandwiches washed down by tea. I knew better than to refuse them, but I could feel the chewed lumps lodging in my throat. Only the liquid from the thermos seemed to give enough moisture for me to swallow.

At nightfall we finally pulled up outside a large grey house. The grass of its small front garden was unadorned by flowers. Instead there was a large sign advertising the fact that it had vacancies for bed and breakfast. This, my parents explained to me, was where we were to stay for the night before my mother took me to my godmother's. After I had my supper, which the landlady served us in a small, bleak dining room, I went listlessly to bed. This was a put-you-up in my parents' room, which I crawled into and fell instantly to sleep.

The following morning, after I'd washed and dressed, I had my breakfast in the same cheerless dining room, and then, with my mother holding my case, we left for the bus, with me trailing despondently behind her.

On the hour-long bus journey my mother kept up a

one-sided conversation. Knowing her as I did, I recognized that her bright tones hid a nervousness. She told me that my godmother was looking forward to my visit. She asked me to be good. She reassured me that our separation would not be for long, and that I would be happy there.

Unbelieving, I sat and listened, giving little response, until gradually her bright chatter became stilled, finally stopping altogether. I felt my fate was the same as the dogs'. I was being re-homed. I could and would not understand why, when my parents were going to live such a short distance away, I could not be with them. As I sat on that bus I anticipated a dislike for my godmother and when we reached her house, I knew I was not going to be disappointed.

After the warm red bricks of Cooldaragh, the grey semi-detached house seemed completely cheerless. I looked with distaste at the tiny front garden with its dark pink hydrangea bush planted in the small patch of dark soil. As my mother raised the iron knocker to announce our arrival, I glanced at the net-curtained windows that hid any view of the interior. I saw the one on the upstairs window twitch, but I couldn't see the occupant. I heard footsteps descending the stairs, and then she opened the door and, with a thin smile, beckoned us in.

My grown-up self has learnt understanding and compassion. I now would have seen a lonely middle-aged woman with few social graces, who was unused to children. To my prejudiced child's eyes, her tall bony frame looked witch-like. My opinion was formed.

My mother and I were seated in her austere sitting room, on her functional upright chairs with their pristine arm caps. A few minutes later the obligatory tea tray arrived, without which no adult conversation seemed able to take place.

As I balanced a small plate, on which sat a dry scone, on my knees, and awkwardly held my china cup, she and I appraised each other. Whereas I saw a witch, she, I am sure, saw a sullen unsmiling child, tall for her age and too thin. The antipathy I felt, I saw reflected in her eyes.

I listened to the two women talking about me, as though I was an inanimate object. For the first time I felt real resentment towards my mother as I sat in depressed silence.

How could she, I thought, leave me here?

I heard their conversation cease, could feel an awkward pause, broken by my godmother's voice saying, 'I'll leave you two alone then, to say your goodbyes,' as she abruptly rose to remove the tea tray.

My mother and I looked at each other warily as I waited for her to make the first move. Finally she opened her handbag, removed an envelope and handed it to me.

'Antoinette,' she said quietly, 'I've got to go now. I've put some pocket money in here for you. It's to last until I fetch you.'

I stood there, numb, as she gave me a quick hug before hurriedly leaving. When I heard the front door close I went to the window. Pulling the net curtain aside I watched her forlornly until she was out of sight. She never looked back.

Anger and resentment consumed me. I missed Judy

unbearably. At night tears oozed down my cheeks as I thought of the fate of the animals. I was being punished but I didn't know what for. I hid my deep unhappiness behind a sullen face in the house and my godmother, with her lack of any experience of children, did not understand that the child before her was disturbed. She just saw a rebel.

Within my parents' house my growing instability had not shown, for they acted as the lid, keeping the pressure in. There I was controlled, emotions were suppressed and behaviour programmed. Now, without those perimeters, my security had gone. An animal that has been trained through fear will revert to bad behaviour when the fear is removed. I was not a child who had been moulded with praise and affection, where confidence was encouraged to grow. I was a child whose night-times were wracked by nightmares and whose daytimes were confusing. A child who not only missed everything that was familiar, but was scared she had been left for ever. Never having been given the independence of being in control of my own emotions, I now felt even more insecure and any rules my godmother tried to enforce were resented.

My parents were my masters; my father controlled me with threats and my mother with her pained manipulation of my feelings. Now anger became the predominant emotion that coursed through my body. Anger was my defence against unhappiness and my godmother became the target for it. She would look on helplessly as I, determined not to give her an inch, rebelled against every one of her commands.

'Don't run, Antoinette,' she would say as we left church,

so I ran. 'Come home straight from school.' I dawdled. 'Eat your greens,' and I would push my food around my plate until she excused me from the table and I was free to go to my room and read. She wrote to my mother saying I was unhappy and she thought it would be best if I went back to her. My mother, who I think had hoped my godmother would grow fond of me and want me to stay, arranged to collect me.

Later I found out that my godmother had felt such a failure in her childcare duties that she had blamed herself, not me, for my behaviour. The result of that was that she refrained from reporting my bad behaviour to my mother, thus saving me from punishment.

I was happy to leave the house, which I had felt was so cheerless. I couldn't wait to wave goodbye to the old woman who I knew had never wanted or liked me. Maybe if I had been able to see into the future and had known what the next few years would bring I would have had second thoughts, but at eleven I knew nothing.

Chapter Thirteen

On the journey from Tenterden to Old Woking, which we made by bus and train, my mother told me about the house that she and my father had bought, and how she had decorated it.

In the 1950s, before patios became fashionable, houses had back yards where there was an outside lavatory, a washing line and, most probably, the husband's bicycle leaning against the unpainted brick walls. However, my mother, who had loved the flowers at Cooldaragh, had seen a picture of a cottage in France and had tried to copy the exterior as much as possible.

She had painted the walls white, the doors and window frames blue. Not only were there window boxes at the front of the house, but also boxes had been firmly tied to the top of the walls surrounding the back yard, which she had filled with nasturtiums. She told me how their tumbling orange flowers contrasted vividly with the newly painted white walls.

The inside of the house, she told me, still needed to be decorated. Her idea was to remove all the wallpaper, paint the kitchen yellow and the rest of the house cream, whilst parquet lino would transform the downstairs floors.

As my mother explained every detail, I could see that she took an enormous delight in planning our new home, the first one they had managed to buy after nearly twelve years of marriage.

At the end of our journey, we walked a short distance to a street, where small, drab semi-detached and terraced houses came straight up to the pavement and not a hedge or bush broke the monotony. Our house stood out bravely with its freshly painted walls, the colourful window boxes and blue door, its brass knocker shining.

That evening when my father came home from work, we all ate supper together. Both of them seemed so happy to have me back that I took courage and told them my news.

'I'm called Toni now.'

My godmother had told me that Toni was the correct abbreviation for Antoinette. Toni, I felt, was my name, the name of a girl who might be popular. Antoinette was someone else.

My mother smiled at me. 'Well, it will be easier to put on your name tags when you start your new school.'

This was her way of voicing her acceptance.

My father made no comment and stubbornly refused to call me Toni until the day he died.

Over the weekend my father was working, so I helped my

mother by stripping wallpaper. First I would soak it using a wet cloth. Then I would take the scraper and peel off long strips. I managed to completely strip the walls that Saturday. I felt close to my mother again. She kept telling me how useful I was being. We had afternoon tea together outside in our flower-filled yard where she answered my unspoken questions.

'Your father is going to visit your grandparents in two weeks, then he will bring Judy back,' she reassured me. 'I'm taking you to your new school on Monday, where you'll meet your headmaster.'

I realized that this was not going to be a girls' only school, which I had become used to again, but a mixed one.

'What will I wear?' I asked.

'Oh,' she answered, 'the headmaster has given permission for you to wear your old school uniform until you outgrow it.'

My happiness at the news that Judy was coming disappeared. My heart sank, for yet again I was going to be dressed differently from the other children.

Sunday came and went too quickly for me. On Monday my mother took me to my new school. That morning, I carefully dressed in my green gym tunic, white shirt and green and black tie, knee-length grey socks, old lace-up shoes, and finally pulled on my green blazer.

When I arrived I shrivelled inside. In the playground were girls in grey skirts, white blouses and ankle socks, their feet enclosed in slip-on shoes. I could see clusters of children of my age playing, groups of teenagers talking together and my confidence plummeted. Armed only with my new name, I followed my mother into the building to meet my new headmaster.

Looking at my school reports, he asked me about my last two schools and what I had enjoyed most there. He questioned me on my hobbies, but how could I explain to him, a town dweller in England, what country life in Northern Ireland had been like? He took me to my classroom and introduced me to the teacher in charge. I saw not the black-gowned figure I was used to, but a large blonde woman with a pretty face. She told me she was taking the English class that day. I was handed a book to read, which I had already studied in Northern Ireland. I realized even my favourite subject was going to be boring.

As class followed class that day I became increasingly despondent because the curriculum was so unfamiliar to me. Breaks came and went. The confident pre-teens in their casual uniforms seemed to be ignoring me. I must have seemed very strange to them in my gym tunic, with my long socks held up by garters, my hair parted neatly and held in place with a slide, whilst theirs was caught up in ponytails. I stood in the playground clutching my books, trying to will just one girl to speak to me.

Not one did.

That afternoon I walked home, watching the other children chattering in groups. To them I no doubt seemed aloof. I, with so few social graces, was an outsider.

At home my mother happily announced that she had found

a job and, two weeks after I started school, my father went to Northern Ireland to visit his family and to bring Judy back. Over the next few weeks I learnt that I had to take an exam called the 11+, something I had been unaware of. The teachers gave me extra homework to bring me up to date with the English curriculum, but with only a few weeks to go I was having sleepless nights.

Although my father was indifferent to my education, my mother certainly seemed to want me to pass. The teachers were confident in me, but I was not so sure. I had mixed feelings over the next couple of weeks, wavering between excited anticipation of Judy's return and dread of the approaching exam.

They both arrived. First, Judy, who shook with joy when she saw me. Although she now had no woods and fields to search around in her quest for rabbits, she soon settled down to her life in the town and her walks on a lead, which I gave her three times a day.

I missed my old school and a lot of my life at Cooldaragh. It seemed that Judy was adapting better than I was.

Then the dreaded exam came; the papers were handed out in silence to the young pupils who all knew how important this day was. I knew I had done well in two of my papers, but the arithmetic seemed very different to me. I looked up despondently at my teacher, who was looking over my shoulder at my answers but said nothing.

After the bell went and all the papers were handed in, I felt despair, for I knew if I failed I would not get into grammar school and would have to stay in the senior section of this school for ever.

During the following few weeks, as I was waiting for the results of the exams, I saw little of my father, who seemed to be working all hours; or so my mother told me. I would come straight home, help with housework, then settle down to do my homework.

Then my father changed his shifts from daytime to night-time. At the same time my mother started work. As the office where she worked was a bus journey away and my school only a few minutes walk away, she left the house before me. On the first morning of our new routine I had my breakfast quickly while a saucepan of water heated on the stove for me to take upstairs to my bedroom for my morning wash.

As only a minuscule landing separated my parents' bedroom from mine, I tried to climb the stairs as quietly as I could so as not to wake my father, who on his return from his night shift had gone straight to bed.

I poured the water into an old china bowl, removed my nightdress, took my flannel and started soaping myself, noticing for the first time as I looked into the mirror that my body was beginning to change. Small breasts were forming on my previously flat chest. Still looking in the mirror I ran my hands over them, not sure if I really liked the changes. Then I saw another reflection.

My father, dressed only in his sweat-stained vest and underpants, had come out of his bedroom and squatted down on the floor outside my door, which he must have opened very quietly. With a smile on his face, he was just watching me. I could feel tremors of fear in my body as I tried to grab the towel to cover myself.

'No, Antoinette,' he instructed, 'I want to watch you. Turn around.'

I did as I was told.

'Now wash,' he commanded.

As I obeyed him I felt a hot flush of shame spread across my face. Then he rose up, came over to me and turned me around to face the mirror.

'Look in the mirror, Antoinette,' he whispered.

While his hand stroked my small budding breasts, his breath rasped in my ear and his other hand slid downwards. Then he let me go.

'You come straight home from school now. Bring me a nice cup of tea when you get in. Antoinette, do you hear me?' He asked as I stood mutely looking at the floor.

'Yes, Daddy,' I whispered.

Then he left my room abruptly, giving me a wink as he went. Still trembling, I quickly dressed, brushed my hair and went downstairs to give Judy her morning walk before I left for school.

That day I was even quieter than usual at school, no longer being the first to put my hand up to answer the teacher's questions, for I knew what was going to happen to me when I went home and made my father's tea. When the bell rang at four o'clock, I slowly packed my satchel and walked home alone, ignoring my peers who were doing the same journey in small groups. But they, I knew, were going to be greeted by caring mothers, because 'latch-key kids' were not common until several years later.

Using my key, I let myself in and was greeted by an excited Judy, waiting for me, as she did every day, to take her for her walk. That day I could feel his presence upstairs even before he spoke.

'Antoinette, is that you?' he called down the stairs.

I answered that it was.

'Well, make me a cup of tea and get yourself up here. Put that dog of yours in the back yard.'

I went through the routine of putting the kettle on the stove, warming the pot for a few minutes, putting the leaves in, letting it brew slowly, adding milk and sugar to the cup, all the time feeling his impatience and my mounting dread. Finally I could delay no longer. I put the teacup on a tray with two digestive biscuits and carried it up to him. As I entered the dark bedroom, where the curtains were drawn, he was lying in the bed that he shared with my mother. Once again I could smell his body odour and sense his excitement. I put the tray beside his bed.

'Go take your gym slip off, and come back in here,' he said as he picked up his cup of tea.

I came back in my vest, knickers, shoes and socks.

'Take them off now,' he instructed, pointing at my vest and school-uniform knickers. Then he lit a cigarette and gave me that smile that I knew so well. Beside the bed was the jar of vaseline that was normally on the dressing table next to his hairbrush. He dipped the fingers of one hand into it while still puffing on his cigarette. I could feel the fear inside me, for I knew my mother would not be home for two hours, and I could sense that what had happened to me in Northern Ireland was going to be worse now. I knew that my changing body was exciting him more than my younger one had.

He pulled me onto the bed so I was sitting across his knees. Taking his fingers out of the jar, he roughly forced them into me. Then he got out of the bed and positioned me as he always had in the car all those years ago, legs dangling helplessly over the edge of the bed. He entered me more roughly than ever before. I could close my eyes, but not my ears.

'You like this, Antoinette, don't you?' he whispered.

When I didn't answer he pushed harder and my whole body went rigid with pain.

'Now tell your Daddy you like it,' he said as he took a final puff on his cigarette. 'Say "Yes, Daddy, I like it".'

I obeyed in a whisper. Then I felt that sticky substance dripping onto my thighs as, still holding the end of his cigarette, he spurted over me.

'Now go and clean yourself up and tidy up downstairs before your mother comes home from work,' he told me as he pushed me roughly off the bed.

I dressed in an old skirt and jumper, went down to the lavatory in the back yard and rubbed and rubbed myself with damp toilet paper, trying to remove the stickiness and the smell of him. Then I went inside to clean out the ashes left in the fire from the night before, laying a new one using rolled-up newspaper and small pieces of wood to get it going. I brought coal from outside, washed up and, a few minutes before my mother was due, put the kettle on the stove so that she could have fresh tea waiting for her.

Chapter Fourteen

Dimly I heard my mother's voice calling up the stairs, penetrating the waves of pain that lurked behind my eyes, pain that gripped the top of my head while invisible claws squeezed into the back of my neck.

It was time, I knew, to go downstairs and collect water for my morning wash. I opened my mouth to call out to my mother but only a rasping croak left my lips. My eyes felt glued together as if to protect them from the glare of the morning light as it burned painfully through my lids. Raising a hand that overnight had become heavy, with fingers that were swollen and stiff, I tried to rub them, only to feel the burning heat from my forehead.

Forcing my body to sit up, dizziness made the room spin, black dots danced in front of me and sweat trickled down from my forehead. Icy cold, with shuddering body and chattering teeth, panic made my heart beat faster, until I could hear the blood pounding as it coursed through my body.

I lifted my legs out of bed and staggered to the mirror. A stranger's face stared back at me, a stranger with yellow-tinged skin stretched tightly over a puffy face. Dark shadows had appeared overnight to circle my eyes, while lank, damp hair lay plastered to my head. Again I raised my hand to my head to sweep the hair away and noticed that the fingers were as yellow as my face and swollen to twice their normal size. Trembling, I climbed down the stairs on legs that felt too weak to support me and fell onto a chair. Tears fell unchecked down my cheeks as I saw my mother's cold stare.

'What's wrong now, Antoinette?' I heard her ask, and then a note of concern crept into her voice. 'Antoinette, look at me.' Her hand touched my forehead briefly. 'My God,' she exclaimed, 'you're burning up.'

Hastily telling me not to move, not that I thought there was any possibility of that happening, I heard her cross the room into the small hallway where the telephone was kept. She dialled and spoke rapidly into the phone.

A few minutes later she came back with a blanket, which she wrapped gently round my shoulders and informed me that the doctor was on his way. How much time passed I couldn't tell as I descended into a temperature-induced daze. I sat alternately shivering one moment, burning up the next. I was aware of a knock on the door and the voice of our local doctor and I felt a sense of relief, sure he would help me.

A cool thermometer was placed in my mouth, fingers held my wrist and all the time the figures in front of me blurred.

The doctor informed my mother that I had a temperature of 103, and that I had inflammation of the kidneys. 'Nephritis,' he called it, insisting on phoning for an ambulance immediately.

I heard the vehicle come, felt my mother holding my hand on the journey but hardly felt being carried on the stretcher to the children's ward, nor being placed on the bed to await an examination. I just wanted to sleep.

The next few days are only a dim memory, a blur of feeling constantly sick, of sharp needles injecting into my buttocks a substance that later I would learn was penicillin, of hands turning me over and a damp cloth periodically wiping my feverish body. Other times my sleep would be interrupted when my head was held and a straw placed into my mouth, allowing cool liquid to trickle down my parched throat, or when a cold metal bowl was slid under my bottom and voices told me not to sit up, but to lie flat until I was stronger.

Those first few days seemed to roll into one, where only the ministrations of the nurses punctuated my sleep. Visiting time would be the only hour that I felt the necessity of keeping my eyes open.

The children around me would watch the double doors at the end of the ward, staring impatiently at the clock as the hands crept slowly round to the hour when the doors would swing open to admit a stream of smiling adults carrying gifts of toys, books and fruit.

My head would turn on the pillow, my eyes fixed to the

doors, straining to look for my mother. She, on the doors being opened, would rush to my side in a cloud of perfume, sit by my bed, hold my hand, brush the hair from my face and kiss me in a public display of affection. My father's smile as he gazed at me showed his concern, while the smile he flashed at the nurses won him answering beams from them.

I'd worried her, my mother told me, given her such a fright. However, now I was in good hands and must be a good girl and get better. I was, she explained, to stay in the hospital for several weeks, in fact not only in hospital but in bed. She went on to tell me that I had a very severe kidney infection and that I was only allowed a diet of glucose and barley water. She said that the house was quiet without me, that Judy missed me and she knew I would get better as soon as I could. Looking up at her from my prone position while she talked, my eyes would focus on her face until the force of my father's stare would draw them away to meet his.

The smile on his lips was always the smile of the nice father, but in his eyes I could see the nasty one, the one invisible to everyone else, the one that lived inside his head.

As the days became weeks my strength gradually returned and with it an interest in my surroundings. Although still confined to bed, I could sit up against the pile of pillows, which had increased from one to three over the same number of weeks. Now that my eyes had ceased their droopy tiredness, reading became a pleasure again. Twice a week I eagerly awaited the trolley bearing suitable books. On the first visit, when I'd informed the visiting librarian that my favourites were detective stories, I received a look of dismay at such an unchildlike taste and a tut of disapproval. However, we settled on Agatha Christie's stories of the antics of Tommy and Tuppence, followed by Miss Marple and Hercule Poirot. Luckily for me, Agatha was a prolific writer and my supply seemed inexhaustible.

The unvarying routine of the ward brought its own comfort. First the early morning round of bedpans for those children confined to bed. There we would perch, straining away like rows of battery hens, knowing that the contents of these cold metal containers were going to be scrutinized before being wheeled away. Next would come bowls of water for our morning 'top and tail' wash, when for modesty's sake the curtains would be drawn around us.

Breakfast followed. Protein-rich eggs and brown bread served to the nearby beds would make my taste buds moisten but I received only my cup of pale grey, viscous glucose.

Only after the trays were removed could I reach for my book and search for the solution to mysteries before the current detective had effortlessly revealed the culprit.

I was scarcely aware of the constant hum of activity of the busy ward around me. The swish of the nurses' blue and white uniforms, the soft tread of their white lace-up shoes on the grey industrial flooring, the chatter of children recovering and the metallic tone of the curtain rings as they were drawn round the bed of a child sicker than I all blended into the background as, engrossed, I turned the pages.

Lunchtime smells would assail my nostrils, my deprivation

of any protein meaning that all food smelt good. I would gaze enviously at the trays as my glutinous drink was served to me.

'Drink it up, Antoinette,' would be the cheerful command as I stared mutinously at the unappealing liquid. 'It will do you good.'

I wanted food.

'It will make you better, and then you can go home.'

I wanted cake, ice cream, sweets and a plate piled high with brown toast, dripping with yellow butter, mixed with swirls of dark brown Marmite. Pictures of such treats floated in front of my eyes as my mouth watered with memories of their tastes. Then I spooned the unappealing mass in my cup into my mouth, forcing myself to swallow. The effort of getting better, with its starvation diet and the endless pricking of needles, appeared an arduous and lengthy journey.

After lunch came bed making, where the sheets were straightened so tightly that they left us immobilized. Then, with arms tightly bound and neatly combed hair, we would await matron's rounds.

The double doors would burst open and a stately presence would sweep in, followed by an entourage of doctors, a blue-clad ward sister and a staff nurse. A starched ruffle would keep matron's formidable white-capped head erect, her cape swinging behind her. She paused imperiously at the end of each bed to ask each mummified child how they were feeling.

On hearing, 'Very well, thank you Matron,' she would proceed to the next bed until her round was completed. Then the doors would once again open and, with her regal exit, a collective sigh of relief would emit from both staff and patients. Arms would wriggle out of bedclothes; bodies would slide down into comfortable positions as the afternoon nap that preceded visiting hour began.

Night-times always came too soon for me; they always interrupted my detective unmasking the most unlikely person in the book to be the villain, but, much as I resented my adventure by proxy being halted, I usually fell quickly into a mostly uninterrupted sleep. Only the rare admission of a night-time patient would disturb me. It was on one of those occasions that I saw the baby.

I heard the slight rattle of the curtain hooks two beds away from me, opened a sleepy eye and saw a small form with, in my child's mind, the head of a monster. A head completely bald and so large that any movement, I felt, could have snapped its fragile neck. An overhead lamp cast a dim orange glow onto the cot. A woman leant over it, her hand touching the baby's tiny fingers, then the curtains rattled again as they were closed and I fell back into a restless sleep.

For two days the curtains around that bed remained shut as both nurses and doctors eased themselves in and out, keeping the sight of what was in there away from our eyes. On the third night, as though in a dream, I saw the woman again, and knew by her posture that she was grieving. I saw a bundled form being held in the arms of the ward sister as she carried it through the doors, saw the light go out and then my eyes closed.

The next morning the curtains were drawn back, an empty cot was neatly made up and of the baby there was no sign.

With that instinctive knowledge children sometimes have, I knew it was dead. I also knew not to ask about it.

Each afternoon I watched the children looking at the doors as they waited for their families with excited anticipation. I saw their faces light up, saw their arms rise for their hugs, heard their squeals of excitement and felt my own flicker of dread. Lying in that hospital bed I could not avoid my father's eyes nor the fear I felt of him.

Six weeks after my admittance he arrived alone. Memories, which the gentle routine of the hospital had partly diminished, rushed back into my mind and my fingers grasped the sheets tightly.

I wondered where my mother was, as he took my hand and leant over to kiss me on the cheek. In answer to my unspoken question he told me that she had a bad cold and didn't want to bring her germs into the ward. His thick wavy hair gleamed with brilliantine that day and his smile sparkled at the nurses. But the nasty father lurked in his eyes and slid out of his mouth with every word he uttered.

Still holding my hand while I slipped further down my pillows, he said, 'Antoinette, I've missed you. Have you missed your Daddy?'

The puppet me took over. 'Yes,' I whispered and my newly acquired strength seemed to leave my body.

'Well, when you come home, sure I'll have a present for you. You'll like that won't you, Antoinette?'

I didn't ask him what the present was; I knew. I felt the pressure of his hand as he waited for my response. I looked up at him and gave him the answer he wanted.

'Yes, Daddy.'

He beamed at me, and I saw the self-satisfied gleam in his eyes. 'Now you be a good girl, Antoinette. I'll be back tomorrow.' And he was.

The nurses kept telling me what a good father I had, how he loved his little girl, how it would not be too long before I went home.

After his third visit I waited until the other children had fallen asleep. I took the cord from my dressing gown, tied one end around my neck and the other end to the bed head. Then I threw myself towards the floor.

Of course I was found. The night nurse seemed to think I was depressed because I wanted to go home. She repeatedly reassured me that it would not be much longer. She tucked me back up in bed and sat beside me while I drifted off to sleep. The next morning my dressing gown cord had been removed.

That visiting time both my parents came through the doors. My mother took my hand while my father stood with his arms folded.

'Antoinette,' she said, 'I'm sure last night was some mistake. Matron rang me today. Now I'm sure you don't want to worry me like that again.'

I saw the bright smile and knew the incident had been placed firmly into the box marked 'Not to be talked about'.

The game of happy families was still in place and she the central character in the tableau.

'Daddy and I have been talking,' she went on, including him in her smile. 'You're obviously going to be run down when you leave here. So we've decided to send you to Auntie Catherine.' I hardly knew Aunt Catherine, but I had always liked her on our rare visits. 'A few weeks in the country will do you the world of good. We won't talk about this silly business again, dear, and of course we won't mention it to your Aunt Catherine. We wouldn't want to worry her now, would we?'

I felt my father's stare as I looked at my mother, feeling her jerk the cord that bound me to her. Wanting her approval I replied, 'Thank you, that will be nice.'

With their mission accomplished both parents relaxed for the rest of visiting time, then, as the bell announcing its end rang they left with a flurry of kisses. I wiped my chin where my father's lips had landed, then picked up my book and lost myself in the pages.

True to her promise the dressing-gown cord incident was never referred to again. My mother's pattern of tackling problems was already firmly in place: 'If we don't talk about it, it never happened.' As if her denial was contagious, neither did any of the hospital staff.

My father only visited on his own one more time.

'Remember, Antoinette, what I've told you. You don't be talking about our family business my girl, do you understand?'

'Yes, Daddy,' I replied as I slid further down the bed, trying to avoid the glare of his eyes. In their depths I could glimpse the seeds of the rage that would be unleashed should I ever dare to disobey him.

Every day I waited for my mother to come through the double doors again, and was repeatedly disappointed. When at last she made another appearance she was full of apologies. Her excuses drifted around my head and I, wanting to believe her, nodded my head at appropriate times. Work, she told me, had tired her out. Such a long way to come by bus, she continued. She told me that Auntie Catherine was looking forward to my visit, and that because her family were well off she did not need to work. She wished she could afford to take time off to look after me but she knew I would understand why she couldn't. I must be looking forward to my visit as well.

I, at eleven, only knew I wanted to go home to my mother, but my desire to please remained as strong as ever.

'It'll be nice to see Auntie Catherine,' I replied and was rewarded by a brilliant smile and two kisses planted on each side of my face.

The final days in hospital blended into one as I read, played with the other children and waited to be told that the following day was to be the last one there. Finally it came.

I dressed early that morning, packed my small suitcase with the accumulation of books and clothes that I had acquired over the three months I'd spent there. When that task was finished I sat patiently on my bed and waited for my mother.

Chapter Fifteen

My mother had taken me by train and bus to the large rambling house on the Kentish coast where my aunt lived. Here I had been given a pretty room where the wallpaper matched the flower-sprigged eiderdown that covered my white-painted bed. This, I had been told, had been Aunt Catherine's daughter's room, but now Hazel was in her teens she had moved into a larger one so it was to be mine for the duration of my visit.

My Aunt Catherine was not a blood relative, but my mother's closest friend. In the fifties adults' names were often prefixed with the title 'aunt' or 'uncle' to anyone under twenty-one. She was a pretty woman with the shoulder-length hair of a mousy-brown hue that was fashionable then, belonging to a generation that relied little on the artifice of hairdressers' skills. Her evocative perfume, a mixture of a light floral scent and delicious baking smells, lingered in the room after she left it. Her nails, unlike my mother's, were short, varnished with just the palest pink polish, and on her feet she wore flat sandals. High heels, I noticed, were only worn on special occasions, such as days when she took me to tearooms reminiscent of my early childhood.

The first outing I had with her was to a large department store, where she asked me to choose some material.

'You've grown tall in hospital, Antoinette, and so thin that none of your clothes seem to fit.'

Thus she tactfully dismissed my case of hand-me-downs, gratefully received by my mother and greatly despised by me. 'Let's choose something pretty together.'

Taking my hand she led me into the lift where its guardian, a war veteran dressed proudly in the store's uniform, his empty sleeve pinned across his chest, rested against a stool as he recited the goods of each floor until we reached haberdashery. Those were the days of post-war England, before automation made such jobs extinct.

Passing through the section where the buttons, wools and various knitting accoutrements were, we came to the fabric section. Bolts of fabric in every colour of the rainbow met my delighted eyes; colours I'd never seen before. Delicate silver cloth and beaded chiffon caught my attention first. I wanted to rush over and examine them all, but Aunt Catherine gently took my hand and steered me to the more appropriate cottons.

'Look,' she exclaimed as she pulled a delicate pink and white striped roll towards me, 'this will suit you.' Then, before I could answer, she pointed to another pale blue fabric. 'Do you like that one?'

I nodded, scared the spell would be broken. The excitement had stilled my tongue and made me hold my breath.

'Well, then we'll have both,' she exclaimed happily. 'Now, we need one for best.'

She saw my eyes alight on a rich tartan, like the fabric from the favourite dress I had now outgrown.

'We'll take that as well,' she told me. Then, with our purchases wrapped and bagged, she took me to tea. I felt I could die of happiness, not one new dress but three. I trotted along at her side with a smile so wide it almost made my cheeks ache.

Knowing this was a special day, she allowed me a piece of cake, despite my restricted diet. As I swallowed the soft sponge and felt the sweetness of icing on my tongue, happiness enfolded me and I felt I wanted to stay with her for ever.

Entering a life previously only glimpsed before from the conversations of other children, I had gone 'through the looking glass', like Alice, and had no wish to return. That day I forgot about Judy, how much I was missing her, and allowed myself to savour every moment. My obvious pleasure animated Aunt Catherine as she chattered on about different outings she had planned for us.

'We can't do too much,' she warned me, 'because you're not fully better yet, but in a few weeks I want to take all of you to the circus. Would you like that?'

I felt my eyes grow larger; this was a treat I had only read about. I had dreamt about going to a circus but had never been.

'Oh yes!' I managed to squeak. Surely, I thought, this day could not get any better.

Over the weeks I stayed I learnt that making her family happy was what gave Aunt Catherine the most pleasure and I felt part of it. Her two children – Roy, who was one year older than me, and Hazel, five years older – had largely ignored me. Roy ignored me because I was still not strong enough to play and Hazel because of the age difference. So I was surprised, but very pleased, when two weeks after my arrival Hazel offered to show me her horse. Horses were her passion; she'd been riding since she was a little girl and had owned a pony until she outgrew it. Her new horse had been given to her for her fifteenth birthday and was her pride and joy.

He was a gelding, she informed me, a light bay of fourteen hands. She, I learnt, felt about him much as I did about Judy, although she made it clear that whereas a dog was very good to talk to, a horse could be ridden and was therefore more useful.

Aunt Catherine gave us a bunch of carrots to feed to him, warned Hazel not to let me walk too far and, with the beginnings of hero worship forming, I followed her to the field. There a light golden brown horse, a lot bigger than the ponies from Cooldaragh, came trotting up to us. I was told to hold my hand out flat with my offering, which, tentatively, I did. I felt a wave of delight as his soft breath tickled my palm and my confidence grew as he allowed me to stroke his head.

Hazel saddled him up, then to my delight asked if I would like to ride him.

'Oh yes!' was my instant reply. After all, I'd only been told not to walk too far; nobody had said anything about riding.

I had to stretch to gain a foothold in the first stirrup as Hazel held him steady. Then, with one more heave, I was on. Suddenly the ground seemed a long way down, so I looked straight ahead and took the reins. First he walked and I, feeling over-confident, gave him a light tap with my heels, as I had seen riders do. I felt him pick up a little speed and, as I tried to move to his rhythm, he, with all the joy of a young horse, broke into a canter. Wind made my eyes water, my vision blurred and, as I felt my control go, my excitement changed to fear. I heard Hazel calling his name as he cantered round the field. She shouted at me to pull on the reins, but all my efforts were being spent on staying on.

Then, with frisky pleasure, his back legs went up in the air and I flew over his head. My breath left my body in one big huff and for a moment I saw stars, as I lay on the ground with my limbs akimbo and my eyes open but unfocused.

Hazel's worried voice penetrated my haze and hero worship strengthened my spine. I braced myself until the world stopped tilting, then gingerly I stood. Hazel's look of worry lessened as she brushed me down, no doubt thankful that there were no broken bones to be explained away.

To my dismay she said, 'You have to get back on the horse. If you don't you never will, you'll always be afraid.'

I looked at the gelding who, unconcerned at my discomfort, was contentedly munching the last of the carrots, and saw a giant. Hazel reassured me that she would lead him and, not quite believing her, I climbed back on. Hero worship can make brave little soldiers of us all. I was rewarded, for that day she and I became friends as we silently conspired that Aunt Catherine would be happier not knowing of that little adventure.

Life at my aunt's house that summer was peaceful. Being more confined to the house than her two children, I would spend my days either sitting in the garden reading or helping her in the kitchen. In the mornings her sewing machine would be placed on the large wooden table and clothes for all the family seemed to miraculously appear. First though she made my three dresses. I would stand while she, with a mouthful of pins and tape measure in hand, would pin the material into place until only the hem was left to sew, which she did in the evenings by hand.

Lunch would be a light snack, eaten in the warmth of the kitchen, but evening meals would always be served in the dining room.

During the afternoons the sewing would be put away as the preparation for the evening meal began. I would chop vegetables, peel potatoes and make us both cups of tea as she prepared the family favourites of delicious stews and casseroles, except on Mondays when cold cuts of meat from the Sunday joint were served with pickles and mashed potatoes.

Uncle Cecil, Aunt Catherine's husband, a tall slim man with a warm smile and twinkling eyes, the manager of the local bank, would change every evening out of his pinstriped suit into more relaxed corduroys, shirt and a leather-trimmed cardigan he favoured. Then he would relax with a gin and tonic that my aunt poured for them both as part of their evening ritual.

After the second drink was finished we would sit down to our meal. He took his place at the head of the table and she served our supper. This was always a family affair where he would gently enquire of his children's and wife's activities of that day. Not forgetting me, he would ask about my health and comment on how well I was beginning to look.

Often there would be games of cards or board games such as snakes and ladders once the kitchen was cleared, then bath and bed. Every night I was allowed to read for half an hour before my aunt would come to my room, tuck me up and turn out the light, and I would fall asleep with the happy memory of my good-night kiss.

The day we were going to the circus finally arrived. Dressed in my new pink and white dress and white cardigan, I climbed into the back of the car. Roy, with his precisely parted blond hair combed neatly back, wearing long grey trousers and navy blue blazer, sat beside me trying to look nonchalant as I babbled with excitement.

Bright lights illuminated the big top, the queues filled with children, their bright faces reflecting the thrill they felt as they clutched their parents' hands. Entering the enormous tent the smell of sawdust assailed my nostrils as we took our seats on the tiered benches. I was totally enraptured. First came the clowns with their painted faces, their mouths stretched into permanent smiles, followed by the dancing dogs, small black and white energetic creatures with white ruffs around their necks. At the end of their act each dog sat on a small stool, waiting for the round of applause that was their due. All around me I could see children with their eyes huge and cheeks pink with the thrill of the circus, craning forward to see the clowns reappear, then heard the collective gasp as their act was followed by the large cats. With hands splayed on each side of me to keep my balance I strained to sit as high as possible, not wanting to miss a second of their performance. I shared the excitement of other children, holding my breath with them as those big, beautiful, golden creatures jumped through the ring of fire, clapping my hands vigorously as their tamer took his bow, then falling silent as my mesmerized eyes were drawn upwards and my mouth formed an 'oh' with the rest of the audience as the trapeze artists began their incredible flights.

Then came the majestic elephants, each with their trunk holding the tail of the one in front and a baby one bringing up the rear. I waited for the tiny stools to break when, for their finale, they perched their massive rumps on them, sighing with disappointment when they left the arena. Lastly the clowns made their appearance to announce the end of the show. I could hardly move. I felt encased in a magic bubble of pure joy that only childhood brings. Many years later, when I signed a petition to forbid animals being used in circuses I still remembered the magic of that night with rueful nostalgia.

Two weeks later Aunt Catherine told me what she thought was good news. My parents were coming for the weekend and I was to return home with them. I was to have a check-up at the hospital and, provided all was well, I could return to school for the autumn term.

My feelings on hearing this were mixed; on the one hand I missed my mother and Judy, but on the other I had become used to life in a happy household, being well dressed and feeling part of Aunt Catherine's family. Wanting to please her, I put a smile on my face and assured her that I would miss her, but of course I was looking forward to seeing my parents.

The weekend arrived. I heard their car draw up and stood at the door with my aunt as she welcomed them in. There were hugs and kisses, and exclamations about how much I'd grown, how well I looked. That night it was my mother who tucked me into bed and gave me my good-night kiss, a kiss I still felt warming my cheek as I lay in my bed, wondering what the next week would bring.

Chapter Sixteen

The check-up at the hospital had gone well, and I was pronounced fit to return to school, although I was to be excused from all sports and PE classes, as I was not yet considered strong enough for them. That news I received with pleasure; popularity was won at that particular school not by the ability of a pupil in the classroom but by their skill on the hockey field, speed on the netball court and agility in the gym. None of which I excelled at. Now I had a cast iron excuse to escape the lessons I disliked, and the ridicule that inevitably followed.

My mother had taken a short holiday from work to get me settled and for the next two weeks I enjoyed coming home to her. There were always hot, freshly baked scones and a pot of tea waiting for me and, on Fridays, homemade coffee cake, my favourite. But my greatest pleasure was having my mother to myself, being able to chatter to her without feeling the stealthy gaze of my father following me around.

After I'd eaten and played with Judy I sat at the kitchen table with my homework, which was more demanding now that I was in the seniors and had a lost term to catch up on. My mother would prepare supper as I worked, and as I sat in that warm kitchen I wished those days would never end.

I made up my mind then to stand up to my father when my mother returned to work. I would tell him that now I knew what he did to me was wrong. Although I had always loathed what he did to me I had, up till then, accepted it as unavoidable. After six weeks in a happy household I had come to realize just how wrong it was. Instinctively, I had always known that I must not discuss 'our secret', knew that it was a shameful act, but was still too young to see that the shame was his not mine. I felt that if I told people what was going on they would never again see me as a normal child and would in some way blame me.

Lulled into a false feeling of security, I had settled back into school. My reputation for being delicate made me even more of an oddity, but at least the other children left me alone. Their teasing and taunting ceased because after such a long illness the teachers had made it clear that bullying me would not be tolerated.

The last day of my mother's holiday arrived, bringing with it the reappearance of the jovial father. He entered the house, a dazzling smile on his face and a faint smell of whiskey on his breath. I tried not to wince as his hand chucked me under the chin and then slid up my cheek to rest on my head.

'Look Antoinette, I've a present for you.' He unbuttoned the top of his coat to show me a small grey wriggling bundle of fur. Gently prying small claws from his jumper, he held it out and I reached up my arms to take it. The warm little body nestled up to me and the first rumble of a contented purr vibrated from its stomach. I stroked its fur unbelievingly, a kitten of my own.

'He's yours. I saw him in the pet shop and thought I'd get him for my wee girl.' And I, still wanting to believe in the nice father, allowed myself to be convinced that he existed again, and beamed up at him with delight. The little grey bundle was named Oscar by me, given a box lined with an old blanket to sleep in by my mother, and a sniff by Judy. The following morning he was curled up contently by Judy's side, basking in the warmth of her body while she acted with complete indifference.

That week my father commenced night-shift hours and when I came home it was him and not my mother waiting for me. I put my newly found courage into practice: I said 'no'. He smiled at me, then came that wink.

'But you like it, Antoinette, you told me so, remember? Did you lie to your Daddy then? Hey?'

I felt the trap close round me, for a lie found out was punishable by a beating. Speechless with fear and confusion I stood in front of him with my body trembling.

His mood abruptly changed.

'Make your old man a cup of tea,' he commanded and gratefully I made my escape. A few minutes later he was slurping the hot liquid with his eyes narrowed in an expression I could not read but knew did not bode well for me.

'You know, Antoinette, your Mummy and I do it. We do it all the time.' I gazed at him with horror, unable to tear my eyes away from his mocking stare. 'Do you not know yet how babies are made?'

I didn't but I soon did, and he, I could tell, took a delight in seeing my disgust at what he told me. I thought of all the pregnant women I'd seen, women who seemed happy at their condition, and felt a sickness wash over me at the thought that they were party to such a horrible act. Why, the aunt I loved so much must have done it, I thought, at least twice, and my mother. How could they? My thoughts churned in my head and a different fear entered it. My whole perception of adults shifted that afternoon and the last shreds of security, as I knew it, disappeared, leaving me cast adrift, with only bewilderment as my companion.

He told me that I could not get pregnant, as though that was my only fear, but still I said 'no'. He laughed at me.

'Let me tell you something, Antoinette. Your Mummy, she likes it.' Then, seemingly bored with tormenting me, he shrugged his shoulders and turned away.

Had I won the first round, I wondered. Had it really been as easy as that?

No, I had simply won a minor skirmish, not even a battle, and the war was about to begin. The following day I went to my mother's office. I would surprise her I thought, meet her from work and thus avoid my father's taunts; the taunts that had given me a sleepless night as disturbing images scurried around my brain. The more I had tried to eject them, the more stubbornly they clung on as I tossed and turned.

'What a lovely surprise, darling,' she exclaimed as she showed me to a seat where I could wait for her. When she finished her work she looked up, gave me a warm smile and introduced me to her work colleagues as she played the role of proud mother. Then, with her arm round the shoulders of a daughter who wanted to believe in her, she ushered me out.

My father was waiting for us. Somehow, when I had not returned from school, he had guessed where I'd gone and had quickly moved to outwit me. He told my mother there was a film at the local cinema he knew she would like and he'd come to take her there. The cinema was a treat I loved so, thinking I was included, I looked hopefully up at them.

'Well Antoinette, have you done your homework?' he asked, knowing the answer before I replied.

'No.'

'You get yourself back to the house then. Your mother and I will see you later. If you'd wanted to come with us you should have gone straight home.'

He smiled at me as he spoke, a smile that told me I was beginning to lose again.

'Never mind, dear,' my mother added, 'there will be plenty more times. Help yourself to something to eat and make sure you do all your work.'

I turned in the direction of my home while they, engrossed in each other's company, walked in another.

Three days later, when I came home from school, I saw Oscar lying in Judy's basket, completely still. I knew he was dead before I picked him up. His head was at an odd angle and his small body was already stiff when I held him and looked despairingly into my father's face.

'He must have broken his neck when he was playing,' was his explanation, but I didn't believe him.

Years later, when I looked back on that day, I thought that he most probably was innocent, because I never saw him being cruel to an animal. Perhaps that was one act I accused him of wrongly. Believing him guilty weakened me and he, seeing that, seized the opportunity of taking advantage of my grief. He took my hand and led me to the bedroom.

The tears were running down my face and with a note of kindness in his voice, a note that belied his intent, he gave me a small bottle and instructed me to drink. A fiery liquid slid down my throat, making me choke before I felt its warm glow spreading through me. I did not like the sex that followed, but I liked the whiskey.

So at twelve, I discovered that alcohol could dull pain and saw it as a friend. It was only in later years I realized that a friendship with a bottle can overnight turn into a relationship with the enemy.

I woke up knowing that something good was going to happen. My mind, still dormant, searched for what it was and then excitement flooded my body. My English grandmother was coming to visit. She was going to stay with us for several weeks, sleep on the bed settee downstairs and be there to greet me every day when I returned from school. And the best part of all, during her visit my father would not dare come near me. For the duration of her stay the nice father would be on show and my mother could play her game of happy families.

I stretched with pleasure, thinking of the freedom the next few weeks would bring, and then reluctantly dressed for school. I wanted to be at home to greet her, instead of which my father would be. However, as he did not see her visits giving him freedom, in fact rather the reverse, I knew there was another bonus. He would, as he had done before, swap his shift to a daytime one, so I would have to see much less of him.

For once at school I found it difficult to concentrate and the hours ticked away slowly. Eager to go home, I waited impatiently for the final bell. On hearing it I rushed through the gates and walked as quickly as I could to our house.

I called out to her as I went in and she came with a smile of love on her face and her wide-open arms embraced me.

With her upright stance and feet always encased in high heels, I'd always thought of her as being tall, but as I hugged her I was suddenly aware of how tiny she was. In my flat, lace-up school shoes, I found that my head already reached higher than her shoulder.

Sitting at the kitchen table a few minutes later as she poured out tea I studied her face through the cloud of smoke that always seemed to surround her, a tipped cigarette permanently glued to her lip. As a young child I had watched in fascination, waiting for it to fall, but it never did.

It had been several months since her last visit and I saw that more fine lines were appearing on her porcelain skin and that nicotine had placed a yellow streak in the front of her now faded red-gold hair. Her smile, still full of warmth, which I felt was a special one reserved just for me, flitted across her face as she fired numerous questions; questions about my health, school and what plans, if any, I had made for when I left.

I reassured her about my health, told her I was now fully recovered, even though I was still unable to take part in sports. I said that although I didn't like my school, my marks were constantly high, and I confided in her my ambition, the ambition of going to university and becoming a teacher of English.

For the next hour her bone china cup was constantly raised to her lips as we talked. Our conversation was only interrupted by the boiling of more water for our numerous refills. I remembered as I watched her drink how she had repeatedly told me the only china a teacup should be made from was the bone thin kind, infuriating my mother when she proceeded to take her own cup from her bag and place it on the table.

I was fascinated by its prettiness and had stared at it with admiration the first time she had held it up to the light, amazed that I could see the outline of her fingers through it. I wondered how such a delicate object could be strong enough to resist cracking when she filled it so many times with the almost black, boiling hot tea she favoured.

Now that my grandmother was at home, my parents acted as though a permanent baby-sitter had arrived and their nights out, usually to the local cinema, became more frequent. I didn't tell her that my parents would have left me on my own had she not been there, although not so often that the neighbours might have noticed. If ever my father's violent temper towards me failed to scare my mother, the prospect of gossip always succeeded.

My parents would exit in a swirl of instructions directed at me – to finish my homework, to be good, to go to bed when my grandmother told me – followed by a quick kiss from my mother. A bright, 'See you in the morning, darling', would emit from her carefully lipsticked mouth. Then the door would close behind them, leaving my grandmother and I glancing furtively at one another; me wondering what she thought of my being ignored, and she wondering how much I minded.

Those evenings my grandmother and I spent playing cards. Now that I had left children's games such as snap behind I happily progressed to gin rummy and whist. Some evenings board games such as snakes and ladders or Monopoly would appear out of her case. The hours would flash by as, determined to win, I would silently concentrate on the moves I had to make. She, with apparently equal determination, would squint through the smoke of her precariously dangling cigarettes.

Bedtime would arrive all too soon and a last hot drink would be swallowed before I climbed the stairs and fell into bed. Always she would give me thirty minutes before following me up. There would be a hug and I would breathe in the scent of face powder mixed with her 'lily of the valley' fragrance, which, over the years, had become almost masked with the familiar odour of cigarettes.

Only once in my presence did she show her disapproval of my parents. They, dressed up again for their evening outing with that glow between them that made them a couple, never a family, mentioned the title of that night's film. It was a Norman Wisdom one that I had heard my classmates talking about and wanted to see. My expression must have shown the hope I felt, hope that just once I would be included. My grandmother saw it and tried to help.

'Why, Ruth,' she said to my mother, 'that's a "U"-rated film. Don't worry about leaving me alone – tomorrow's Saturday so Antoinette can go with you if you like.'

My mother froze for a moment before gathering her thoughts and answering lightly, 'Oh, not this time, she has homework to do.' Then she turned to me with a promise that I no longer trusted. 'There'll be other times, darling,' she said in a voice that was meant to console me but didn't, ruffled my hair and was gone, leaving me sitting desolately behind.

'That's not right,' I heard my grandmother mutter. 'Still, cheer up Antoinette,' and with that she put the kettle on to make me an extra cup of tea.

She must have said something to my parents for the next night they stayed at home and when it was time to go to bed it was my mother who came to tuck me in, not my grandmother. She sat on the end of the bed, the role of caring mother firmly in place, a role that she completely believed in.

'Your grandmother tells me that you were upset last night that we didn't take you with us, but you know we can't take you everywhere we go. I thought it would be nice for you to spend some time with her. It's you she really comes to see.'

'But she comes to see all of us,' I mumbled.

'Oh no, dear, my brother's her favourite, always has been. And his wife is so like her. No, dear, if it wasn't for you I doubt if I would ever see her. So I think it would be selfish to leave her alone. Don't you, dear?'

'Yes,' I answered, for what other answer could I give?

She smiled at me, pleased that I understood. 'So we won't hear any more of this silly nonsense will we dear?' She looked at me for the reassurance she knew would come.

'No,' I finally whispered, and with a fleeting kiss that hardly touched my cheek she left me in the darkness to fall asleep thinking how selfish I'd been towards the grandmother I loved.

The next time they went out I told my grandmother that it had only been that one film I wanted to see and that my mother would take me to see a Norman Wisdom film in the school holidays. I was happy they'd left us because I loved spending time with her, I assured her. That part was true, but I still did not like being excluded. I knew it was another sign of how little I was loved. I think my grandmother did too, but she appeared to accept my words at face value and later we happily played a game of gin rummy. A game I won, which suggested she was not concentrating as much as she should have been.

That night she made me a milky drink of cocoa and gave me an extra biscuit. The next day she was waiting at the school gates. She informed me she had decided to take me out for tea and had told my mother that I would do my homework later.

Proudly, I took her arm. She was dressed in her smartest blue tweed coat with a small blue hat perched jauntily on her head. I wanted the other children to see I had a relative, one who not only cared for me, but was also so pretty.

I was rewarded the following day when my classmates remarked on how nice my mother looked. I took great pleasure in their astonishment when I told them that the pretty red-haired woman they had seen me with was my grandmother.

The weeks with her sped quickly by and all too soon it was time for her to leave. Seeing my woebegone face on the morning of her departure, she promised me that her next visit would not be too long away; in fact she had made her mind up that she would visit before my summer holidays. That seemed too far away for me because the Easter holidays were looming up and even the release from the school I hated could not compensate for the three weeks I knew I would be back in my father's power. Weeks when

I knew he would change back to the nightshifts and I would have little escape.

Chapter Seventeen

The last day of term I was surrounded by the excited babble of my peers. Plans were being made for meeting up, and there were discussions about the fun they were going to have in their weeks of freedom. For once I was pleased not to be included, for what could I have said?

On her departure my grandmother had pressed some notes into my hand, with instructions to buy something for myself. Then, to make sure I did, she told me to write to her and tell her what it was. I had already decided: I wanted a bicycle and I knew where there was one for sale. I'd seen a card pinned in the local shop, informing anyone who was interested that a lady's bicycle was being offered for £2 10s. Now I had the money I was determined to buy it. In my head I could see myself cycling to school after the holidays and parking it next to the other ones.

A quick phone call informed me that it was still available, so on the first day of my holiday I walked to the given address.

The transaction only took a few minutes and then I was riding it triumphantly away. The front wheel wobbled dangerously with my inexperienced pumping of the pedals but within an hour I had mastered the intricacies of the three gears and my balance. Delighted with the new sense of freedom it gave me, I thought I would cycle into the next town, which was Guildford, and explore the cobbled streets that I had seen when my mother and I had taken the bus there.

I still had money left, so not only could I visit its many second-hand bookshops but my mother's favourite bakery as well. There my mouth would water as soon as I smelt the warm aroma of freshly baked bread. I decided I would purchase one of the crusty loaves that my mother loved and return with it for our tea.

In my head my whole holiday was planned. I would spend time taking Judy for long walks, visit the library where I could pass hours just browsing, and explore the countryside on my bicycle. If I could manage to complete the housework while my father slept I could make my escape from him before he awoke.

Each evening at supper I would tell my mother my plans for the following day and sense the tension within my father. But if I had promised to return from Guildford with the bread she liked, he could not ban me from going. Or so I thought.

By the end of the first week of my holiday I became more adventurous, staying in Guildford until the early afternoon. I arrived back happily intending to take Judy for a walk and then make tea for my mother. My happiness quickly evaporated when, as soon as I entered the house, I heard my father's roar of rage.

'Antoinette, get yourself up here.'

Quaking with fear I did as I was told.

'Where have you been, my girl?' he shouted, his face red and contorted with rage. 'I've been awake for an hour, wanting my tea. You pull your weight in this house, do you hear me, Antoinette? You're nothing but an idle lump. Now get down those stairs and make me some tea!'

I shot down the stairs, put the kettle on with shaking hands and looked at the clock. It was gone four o'clock, my mother would be home in just over an hour. It was too late for him to touch me tonight, but I knew that moment had only been postponed.

As soon as the kettle had boiled I hurriedly made his tea, placed a biscuit in the saucer and took it to him. As I went to walk out of the room I heard the menacing tones of his voice.

'Where do you think you're going? I'm not finished with you yet.'

My legs went weak as thoughts spun around my head. Surely he could not mean what I thought, when my mother was due back so soon?

'Pass me my cigarettes, then get yourself down those stairs and get the tea ready for your Mummy. Don't you be thinking you can sit around on your backside all night either.'

He glared at me and I felt terror, knowing his temper was barely under control.

He took my bicycle that evening. He told us it was so that he could get to work faster, giving us his wide smile and a wink as he rode off on my treasured possession. My mother said nothing.

The following morning my bicycle was in our back yard with a flat front tyre, and my first period had started.

Confined to the house with no transport and with cramping pains clawing at my stomach I had no escape, and he showed his fury at being denied his pleasure. First he made me clean the house, then run up and down the stairs with numerous cups of tea. No sooner had I lain down than he called me again. It seemed that he needed very little sleep or, if he did, the desire to torture me was greater. That was the second week of my holiday.

For the last week my grandmother returned and with her return my life changed again, for she had come with a purpose.

I was not happy at school, she had told my parents. She did not believe I could stay there for another six years or I would give up before I got to university. My father, she knew, did not like England so she wanted to help them move back to Ireland. Private school fees were cheaper there and she would pay for me to return to my old school. She would even pay for another uniform. She had noticed I had no friends to leave behind and at least in Ireland there was my father's large family.

My father wanted to return. He missed being with his family, where he was admired and through whose eyes he saw himself as successful, while he knew my mother's relatives saw him as an uneducated 'Paddy'.

My mother agreed, hoping as always that the grass would be greener at the end of a journey. The little house was put on the market and quickly sold, the tea chests came out again and at the beginning of the summer holidays we made our last journey as a family.

I too hoped this would be a new beginning. I missed Ireland and my grandmother was too infrequent a visitor for her love to compensate for the life I had in England. So the three of us, all with different hopes, left England and made the return trip to Coleraine.

Once again my Irish relatives gave us a rapturous greeting. My Irish grandmother stood in the street waiting with tears of joy running down her face. My mother, who disliked any public show of emotion, gave her a stiff hug while I stood shyly by. I now knew that their homes were classed as 'the slums' and their way of life was completely different from what my mother had been used to, but to me the warmth and kindness found there completely outweighed the lack of money.

Seen through older eyes the sitting room was claustrophobically small and over-heated. And the small table covered in clean newspaper screamed poverty. When I went to the outside lavatory I felt touched that there hung a toilet roll, knowing it had been placed there for my and my mother's sake. Pages of newspaper cut into squares were hung on a nail for those with less delicate sensibilities.

My Irish family must have seen me as a younger version of my mother. I spoke like her, I sat like her and the manners of the English middle classes had been drummed into me from birth. Now that I was no longer a small child they must have searched for similarities between my father and me, but they would have found none. They saw the daughter of a woman they tolerated for my father's sake, but never thought of as family. Like her, I was a visitor in their home; loved because of my father but not for myself. I think that was what made their final decision about me two years later so easy.

This was Northern Ireland in the late fifties. This was Ulster, whose small grey towns painted their street curbs red, white and blue and hung banners proudly in their windows.

In my family's home town the male population donned black suits and hats to march on 'Orange Day'. Staunchly Protestant, the residents of Coleraine stood for the national anthem but disliked the English – 'their effete masters across the water'. Northern Ireland was steeped in prejudice and the people ill informed of their own history. Even though their dislike of the English stemmed from tales of horrors during the nineteenth-century potato famine, their history teachers should have told them that many of them had Catholic forefathers who had 'drunk the soup' for survival. It was that reward of thin broth for changing religion that created so many of them. But, to a man, they disliked the

Catholics even more than the English. The Catholics, who had lost so much under British rule and were still seen as second-class citizens, could still have pride in their history. While the families who, like us, could have traced their history back to the chieftains who once ruled Ireland and defended it against invasion did not do so for they had renounced their forefathers. In the years there that I grew from child to young adult, I learnt that religion has very little to do with Christianity.

But it was also a country where the people in small communities looked out for each other. During my father's childhood, when times were hard, food was shared with those who had none. A country that had known years of hardship was also a country, as I was to find out, where a whole community could take a united stand and kindness could be replaced by an unwavering lack of forgiveness. At twelve I did not see any of that; I just saw the place where I had always felt the happiest.

Although I knew my family no longer saw me in quite the same way they had nearly three years before, I still felt love for them. I was delighted when I was told that until my parents found a house of their own Judy and I would stay with my grandparents, while my parents would move in with my aunt in the seaside town of Portstewart. Their houses were too small to accommodate us all together so, once I had been re-enrolled at my old school, my parents left and I tried to blend in to the mean streets of the slum area of Coleraine.

The children were friendly; they seemed to feel more fascinated than aggressive about my differences. Maybe that was because they dreamed of leaving their homes one day and searching for that elusive pot of gold in England. Young as they were, they saw it as a land of opportunity and fired question after question at me. Were the wages as high as everyone said? Was the work as plentiful? As soon as they could leave school they were catching that ferry and going to Liverpool or, if more adventurous, on to London.

Between the children who, with rough kindness, accepted me, and my numerous relatives who did their very best to make me welcome, the weeks I spent there were happy-go-lucky times. I was free to play outside from breakfast to bedtime, take Judy for walks in the park and play cricket, where I developed a skill as a bowler. I would squint my eyes, get that little white ball into focus, then aim it at the wickets drawn on house walls. I achieved two successes, scoring points and knocking opponents out of the game and, most important to the adults, I never missed the wall and hit a window. I would crow with glee at every hit, while my team would thump me on the back and tell me I played well, 'for a girl'.

Yes, that was a happy summer, where Judy forgot she was a thoroughbred and became a street dog, running and playing with the multitude of mongrels that lived in the surrounding streets, and I was never scolded for appearing dirty at suppertime. At the same time I looked forward to returning to school. Would they remember me, I wondered. Would the same girls be there? The answer was yes to both questions.

I settled in straight away, feeling a part of this school. I might not have been the most popular girl in the class, but I was accepted.

Just before my thirteenth birthday, one week after I had started the autumn term, my parents fetched me from my grandmother's house. They had rented a prefab in Portstewart as a temporary home while they looked for a place to buy.

Chapter Eighteen

Although the teachers had little rapport with me, not knowing why but sensing something different in me from my peers, the fact that at the end of term exams I came first in nearly every subject gained their respect. My ambition was to go to university. Education would, I thought, bring me freedom, and without knowing my reasons they realized my ambition.

Since my hospitalization, I was still considered too delicate to take part in physical education classes, so those periods I could use for extra study. This I did in the familiar school library, which housed an extensive range of reference books. Obtaining top marks was important to me; it was the one area of my life that I felt in control of, the one part I felt a pride in.

Dr Johnston, our headmistress, made frequent visits to our classrooms and always acted as an inspiration. She liked to open up the minds of her pupils in different ways. She encouraged us to read about politics and history, listen to music and choose books from the library by authors she recommended. She helped us to form our own opinions and not be shy in airing them.

At the beginning of term, which, unknown to me at the time, was to be my last year of school, she announced a competition. Two lists of subjects had been pinned to the notice board that hung in the large entrance hall. One was considered to be of interest to the under-fourteens, the other for those over. We were told to read through them carefully, choose a subject that interested us, then during the term research and write an essay on it. This we would have to present orally to a panel of teachers as well as the other competitors. The prize was a book token, something I coveted a great deal.

At the break, going to the notice board, I read the under-fourteens' list dismissively. I hadn't read a child's book for several years and all the suggested subjects looked ridiculously childish. Then one of the subjects from the senior list jumped out at me: 'Apartheid in South Africa', part of a continent that I had already formed a fascination for from articles I'd read in encyclopaedias.

I went to the more available Deputy Head to ask for permission to choose that subject instead of anything in the younger category. Patiently she explained that if I chose a senior subject, I would have to compete against girls up to five years older than me. When she could see I was still determined, her patience lessened and she informed me that no allowance would be made for my age. Still I was adamant that I knew what I wanted to do.

She called Dr Johnston over and told her, with a slightly patronizing laugh, what I had asked for. Surprisingly, instead of agreeing with her Deputy, the Headmistress overruled her and said that if I was prepared to work in my free time researching a subject not covered yet at school, I had her permission.

I was pleased with my victory, pleased that for once I had obtained my own way. Unknown to me then, however, I had made an enemy of the Deputy Head, a fact I would suffer from the following year.

As I started my research, my passion for my chosen subject grew. I read how the workforces for the mines were recruited once gold and diamonds were discovered, and based the beginning of my essay on that. I wrote that when the white man discovered gold, he also found that many tons of earth had to be shifted to produce an ounce of this valuable metal. To mine successfully, cheap mass labour was needed, which meant black labour. But what, they asked themselves, would motivate the villagers to work long gruelling hours underground when they had never seen the value of the metal buried in the soil? They had operated a barter system for centuries and currency carried no importance for them. The government then passed a new law, stating that the villages would be taxed. Now that the land no longer belonged to the original inhabitants, neither did the gold, which left them unable to pay their taxes. The only option left to them was to send their young men in droves to work the mines. Wives were separated tearfully from their husbands, children from their fathers. First they were herded into lorries, which took them to the trains to travel, often for hundreds of miles, to face uncertain futures.

How did they feel, those men? No longer could they experience the joy of watching their babies grow, feel the warmth from the smiles of their women folk, or listen to stories told by their elders, stories that had been passed down through the years from one generation to another, keeping their culture alive by informing them of their history.

Nor, at the end of the day, could they contentedly sit to watch with wonder the beauty of the African sky, waiting for the sun to gradually disappear, leaving in its wake a sky shot with shades of the palest pink, highlighted by flashes of scarlet and orange.

Neither could they smell the aroma of food being cooked in black pots, hung over open fires and tended by their women. Lost to them was the security and companionship of their village. The very essence of their lives was gone. Instead, their days were spent working long, back-breaking and often dangerous hours in the dark, hearing the unfamiliar sounds of many tongues, until they returned to their bleak soulless dormitories. Their awakenings were now controlled by their masters, not by the stirring of their village coming to life as the sun rose.

Here they quickly learnt that the pride they had felt when they celebrated the day they had come to manhood was stripped away. They became 'boy' to the white man for ever.

As I read more, I found myself totally opposed to the injustice of apartheid, a system created solely to benefit the white races. First they had claimed the land as theirs. They then controlled the original occupants, restricting their freedom in every sense, from the freedom of movement, to the freedom that the benefits of education can bring. These thoughts and opinions became the basis of my essay when I was thirteen.

Why was I so fascinated by a land that up until then I had known very little about? Looking back, I can see that I identified with the victims, as I saw them, and the control that the Europeans exercised over them. I recognized the arrogance of men who believed they, just by their existence, were part of a superior race. I had already learnt that adults also thought that they were superior to children. They also controlled them, restricted their freedoms and bent them to their will.

The black Africans, like me, were dependent for the food on their plates and the roofs over their heads upon people, who because they were in a position of power abused it. In my case and in many of theirs, cruelty was used to make us feel helpless, and our helplessness made them feel superior.

I visualized the people whose country it had once been, having to ask for passes to visit their families, having to always play a subservient role to their white masters. Masters who in many cases they despised as much as I did mine. I could imagine the despair and humiliation they must have felt, and identified with that. I knew, however, that one day

I would leave home. As an adult there would be hope for me, but for them, I suspected, there was none.

At the end of term the day arrived for my essay to be heard. I walked into the assembly room, where the black-gowned judges sat to the left side. The fifth and sixth formers faced me while the upper sixth, in their smart green skirts and nylon-clad legs, sat to the right.

Conscious of my creased gymslip and my knee socks, I climbed the two steps onto the dais, clutching the essay that I had spent the whole term researching. I was the last contestant that day, being the youngest.

Nervously, I opened the pages and felt my voice waver as I started to read. As the passion I felt for my chosen subject calmed my nerves, I felt the atmosphere in the room change from impatience and amused indifference to interest. Out of the corner of my eye, I saw the judges lean forward to hear me better. As I finished my last sentence, I felt the applause break out before I actually heard it. I knew I had won before Dr Johnston announced it.

A wide smile spread across my face as I stood there, triumphant. The cold stare from the Deputy Head's black eyes could not spoil the joy and pride I felt at that moment.

My headmistress warmly congratulated me as she presented me with my book token, and then more applause broke out as I stepped down from the dais. I had never felt so appreciated.

That afternoon, catching the bus home, feeling warm from the glow that success had given me, I let myself into the empty house, which always felt cold. I stroked faithful Judy's head for a few minutes as I told her about my day, and then opened the door for her to play in the small garden.

My father, who I knew was not working that day, was out. He would, as he always did on his free days, collect my mother and they would return together. I slipped into my routine of changing out of my uniform, hanging my gym tunic up carefully and pulling on an old skirt and thick jumper. I emptied the pot-bellied black stove of the previous night's ashes, and carefully laid a new fire. Once that was lit, I went to the small dark kitchen, where I washed up the dishes from the night before. Finally, I laid a tea tray, so that tea would be waiting for my parents as soon as they came through the door.

Once these chores were done, I would let Judy back in, so that she could sit at my feet as I started my homework. That afternoon I was almost too excited to work. I wanted to tell my mother of my achievement, wanted her to hug me with pride as she had not done for so long.

I heard my father's car draw up and quickly poured the water that I had kept simmering over the tea-leaves in the pot. As they came through the door I started telling them my news.

'Mummy,' I said, 'I've won the prize. My essay came first in the whole school.'

'That's nice, dear,' was her only reply as she sat down to drink her tea.

'What prize was that?' my father asked.

'My essay on apartheid in South Africa,' I almost stammered, feeling my glow fading as I saw his mocking gaze.

'What was the prize?' he asked.

Even as I replied, 'A book token,' I knew with a sinking heart what the outcome was going to be.

'Well, give it to your mother,' he commanded. 'It can go towards your school books. A big girl like you should be contributing.'

As I looked at him, I tried to mask the contempt I felt, for I saw not only my father, but what he represented: the gross misuse of authority. As I watched my mother by her silence agreeing with him, I saw how she pandered to his tyranny. I looked at his smug, complacent face and felt such a wave of hatred that it was all I could do to stand upright. I found myself giving a silent prayer to a God I no longer believed in to bring his life to an end.

Into my head for a fleeting moment came a mental picture of him gone, and my mother and I being happy together. For I still believed that my mother's actions were totally controlled by him. As I watched the mother I adored, I thought that surely her life would be better without him. I saw her fuss around him and then I was aware of an intimate loving smile on her face, one she saved just for him. Smiles like that were never given to me.

That was the moment I finally realized that the reason my mother stayed with him was her desire to do so. She, I suddenly knew, would sacrifice anything to stay with the man she had married, to please him and keep him happy.

That evening I, who for years had always blamed my father and never found fault with my mother, only saw her as weak. She appeared to be a woman who not only had lost the chance of a normal happy life, but someone who had lost herself through the love she felt for my father. I knew then that I was not weak like my mother. My achievement that day had proved it to me. Only by standing up to the Deputy Head for what I wanted had I been able to win. I made a vow to myself, then, that no one would ever control my emotions. I would save love for the children I expected to have and for my animals. I would never allow myself to be made weak by it, never allow anyone to come that close. It was a decision that would cloud my life for many years.

Chapter Nineteen

The mind-numbing routines of the hospice seemed to merge the days into one, and the first ten days slipped away without me really noticing.

Sleep would leave me early as the discomfort of the chair reminded me of where I was. As consciousness arrived before my eyes reluctantly opened, I would listen for my mother's breathing and wonder if during her sleep she had finally relinquished her tenuous hold on life. Half hoping but half dreading the answer, I would force myself to look, only to find her gaze holding mine as she patiently waited for me to awaken.

My help was needed to assist her to the bathroom. With one arm around her shoulder and one under her arm we would shuffle across the two-yard distance. The return from the bathroom would result in another agonizingly slow journey back to her chair, where once seated she would lie back with a sigh, worn out before the day had begun.

Around me I would hear the murmur of voices, the quiet tread of rubber-soled feet, the squeak of an opening door and a radio releasing music into the air as the hospice came to life.

We would wait, my mother in her chair, I on the edge of the bed, for the sound of a trolley. It was the arrival and departure of these inanimate objects, pushed by smiling nurses or kindly volunteers, that marked the passing of the hours.

Four pairs of eyes would open and focus on the doorway as the clatter of the first one was heard. This brought the medication, which nullified any pain that consciousness had woken from its slumber.

The second was the gratefully received tea trolley. With my hands curled around the hot cup I sipped the steaming beverage as I waited for the third one, which brought a brief respite for me and breakfast for the patients.

On its arrival I would make my escape. First to a shower room, where standing under its powerful jet I would feel my tension ease. Second to the lounge where, armed with a mug of strong coffee, I would read the daily newspaper in welcome solitude. Here 'no smoking' signs were not displayed, because to these patients the weed was no longer an issue.

No comment would be made when a yellow-tinged patient removed his oxygen mask to replace air with nicotine, as with trembling fingers he held a cigarette to his bloodless lips and sucked deeply. I would remove a packet from my pocket, then thankfully inhale with a sigh of pleasure. The thought that

I might be in the right place to cure my addiction was banished from my mind as my craving was fleetingly satisfied.

The clatter of the returning trolley would penetrate my solitude. I knew it would be piled high with dishes still covered with the residue of brave attempts at eating when all appetite had gone.

Eagerly anticipated doctors' rounds would follow. As I returned to the ward I would notice how four old ladies with limited time left would visibly brighten in the presence of a good-looking young male. All hope of returning home had faded from their minds: both they and he knew that any chance of a cure had ceased on the day they were admitted. All that was left for them were the daily questions on pain control and the adjustment where necessary of medication. Here, with gentleness and compassion, the last journey was eased.

Minor victories would give me fleeting moments of triumph, like a sparkle in my mother's eyes after I had persuaded her to be wheeled to the visiting hairdresser, massaged with aromatherapy oils, or have her nails manicured by a voluntary beautician. The enjoyment of an hour of being pampered temporarily eclipsed the memory of pain and anticipation of what would inevitably follow.

Afternoons brought my father's daily visit. Neither the nice nor the nasty father appeared, but in their place an old man clutching his gift of flowers, bought in haste from a petrol station more skilled at fuelling cars than in flower arranging. An old man who gazed with both tenderness and hopelessness at the only person he had to the best of his ability ever loved, and who in turn had sacrificed so much to stay with him. His tread slowed and his face saddened as he watched his wife die, little by little, day by day.

The pity I felt for him mingled with my night-time memories, and my past and present collided.

On the eleventh day my mother was too weak to shuffle to the bathroom.

On the twelfth she could no longer feed herself.

As I had pleaded inwardly all those years ago for an adult to read in my eyes the desperate need I had, so I inwardly pleaded now, silently begged her to ask for my forgiveness. Only that, I knew, would help her let go of that gossamer thread that connected her to life.

My father's slow tread would quicken as he approached her bed, a smile that masked his feelings appearing just for her. Their palpable bond was a force that had its own energy, which sapped mine. I saw the lounge as my sanctuary, a book as my companion whilst coffee and cigarettes were my sedatives.

Finally my father came to me. 'Antoinette,' I heard him say with a pleading note in his voice that I had never thought him capable of, 'she's never coming home is she?'

I looked into the tear-misted windows of a tormented soul, where evil lay dormant, replaced by the sorrow at his own impending loss.

Wearily, neither seeking nor wanting this confrontation, I replied, 'No.'

Looking at the grief that showed in his eyes compassion rose unchecked; my mind flew back through the decades to the memory of the laughing, handsome, nice father who so many years ago had met us at the docks. I remembered with sadness how much I had loved him then as he had swung me up in the air and kissed my mother. As though that fleeting moment was frozen in time I saw again how my mother had glowed with optimism, and how over the years her hopes had been eroded. A terrible sadness threatened to overwhelm me as I wondered how two people capable of such love for each other had eventually felt so little for the child they had produced between them.

'I know,' he continued, 'I've done terrible things, but can we be friends?'

Many years too late, I thought. Once I wanted love. I craved it. Now I could never give it to you.

A tear escaped from his eye and slid unchecked down his cheek. His age-spotted hand touched mine briefly and for a moment I relented and simply said, 'I'm your daughter.'

Chapter Twenty

Easter had arrived, bringing an early summer that cast both a golden glow over the landscape and a feeling of optimism in our home. For several weeks my father's temper had remained in check and the jovial man whom his friends and family always saw seemed a constant presence. My mother, made happier by his good mood, was kinder and warmer to me. After all I must be doing something right, for it was always my behaviour that provoked his rages; although she never explained exactly what it was that I did wrong.

Just before the holidays my parents had moved into a home of their own. They had finally found a small house within their price range on the outskirts of Coleraine. My mother now had a job she liked and my father had finally bought his dream car – a second-hand Jaguar that he lovingly polished before driving round to his family to show it off. The stir it made in my grandparents' street brought a flush of pleasure to his face, which the admiration he for ever sought always did.

My mother's contentment reflected in her constant humming of the Glenn Miller melodies made famous in her youth. Since optimism is contagious, I had gone out in search of a job myself that I could take during the three-week holiday. I'd found one at a local bakery. I wanted independence and I wanted my own money.

I felt so proud of myself when my first week's salary was handed to me in a brown envelope and on my day off I bought a second-hand set of encyclopaedias and a pair of jeans. This was the beginning of the era of teenage fashion and I wanted to swap my school uniform for the youth culture one. Slip-on shoes came next and a white blouse followed.

When the Easter holidays came to an end the shop agreed to keep me on for Saturday work. With that promise I knew I could save enough for a bicycle. This time I was determined that my father would not borrow it. As he now had a car he loved so much, I didn't think I had much need to be worried. My parents seemed pleased by my activity and although I constantly dreaded being asked to part with my hard-earned money they, in that period of contentment, never did ask. My mother even admired the clothes I'd bought.

The house felt happier than it had for a long time; I had made friends at school and on reflection I think my parents saw it was important that my life appeared that of a normal teenager. On the outside it was. But on the inside it was still far from normal. I had learnt to like whiskey; a drink that I found dulled pain and gave my spirits a lift. But it also caused a lack of energy. Lethargy disguised as 'teenage moods' and 'that time of the month' became my mother's euphemisms for my increasingly frequent bouts of depression. It broke through the happiness I felt from having friends and the independence of work, making the days grey and the nights, with their recurring nightmares, frightening. Terrifying dreams of being chased, of falling, of being helpless, forced me awake, and I would lie covered in sweat, not wanting to resume my sleep for fear of them returning.

My father's frequent demands now had formed a pattern in my life; a repellent act which I tried to block out of my mind as I swallowed the drink that always followed it. It amused my father that while I wanted none of the first I would always ask for more of the second. It was a request that was usually denied, for he had control of the bottle and doled it out several times a week, allowing my liking for the taste to grow. I was still too young to buy my own supply; that took three years to come.

Sundays started being a 'family outing day'. My father would load us into the car with Judy, now a middle-aged dog, in the back with me. The neighbours would see our happy family unit driving out of our road and turning towards the seaside town of Portstewart. My request to stay behind, only uttered once to my mother, had brought forth such wrath that I never repeated it.

'When your father works so hard,' she had exclaimed, 'and on his one day off he wants to do something nice for us. You're so ungrateful. I'll never understand you, Antoinette.'

And that was most probably one of the truest things she ever said to me.

Once we reached Portstewart a picnic of tea, kept warm in a thermos, and greaseproof paper-wrapped sandwiches would be consumed. After a few minutes of letting the food digest, a bracing walk was taken. Judy, thinking she was still a puppy, ran free, yipping excitedly at every seagull she saw, while I chased after her and my parents slowly brought up the rear.

After every outing my mother would always utter the same command: 'Have you thanked Daddy, dear?' and I would mutter my thanks to the smiling man that I so detested and feared.

In those days, before television was in every house, visits to the cinema were commonplace as family entertainment, certainly they were in ours. I loved films. Every time my parents decided they were going to see the latest one I hoped that I would be invited. Very rarely did it happen.

At fourteen I was still not allowed to venture out in the evenings unless I was baby-sitting for one of our relatives. Sometimes I managed to sneak out to a matinee, under the guise of researching a subject in the library, and I would sit enthralled, treasuring the time stolen for myself.

The Easter holidays had drawn to a close once more when my mother surprised me with an invitation.

'Antoinette, Daddy wants to take both of us out tonight so run up and change,' was her opening remark to me as she returned from work with him at her side.

He had left their bed only an hour before, leaving me still in their room, to fetch her. The moment the front door closed behind him I had washed myself, scrubbing and scrubbing at my teeth and tongue to remove the smell of whiskey before straightening the bed and setting the tea tray. Then, dressed again in my school uniform, I awaited their return. My new clothes I kept for best and, as I had very few others, my uniform was what I wore around the house during term-time; I only changed when we went out.

That afternoon he had been careless with the amount of drink that had poured down my throat because he was in a good mood. He'd had a win on the horses and, as I was to learn later, his burst of good temper had made him careless in more than one area.

Feeling sluggish and slightly sick I quickly changed out of my gym tunic and threw it on the bed; a bed I felt like crawling into and sleeping in. Even the idea of a trip to the cinema was of little interest to me.

The film, one of my father's favourites, was a western, but I could hardly concentrate on the action. A headache that started as a pain behind my eyes had crept down into my neck, making me wince at the blast of the guns every time a fight erupted. I wanted to cover my ears when the volume of the music rose to announce suspense; every new noise felt like knives stabbing into my skull. It was with a sense of relief that I welcomed the lights coming on and the anthem being played. All I wanted was to escape into sleep.

But on our return home my escape was delayed, as I was

sent to the kitchen to make tea for my parents. Over the whistle of the kettle I heard a noise that froze me to the spot with fear. It was a terrible roar of anger coming from my bedroom.

'Antoinette, get yourself up here my girl,' were the words, thickened with rage, that I heard bellowing down the stairs from my father's mouth. Not knowing what I'd done wrong now, I went up, my head still pounding and a sick sensation crawling around the pit of my stomach.

He was standing at the foot of my bed pointing to the offending object, the gym tunic.

'Do you think we're made of money for you to throw good clothes down like that?' he shouted and I saw his fist coming towards me.

Almost tripping in my haste I ducked, turned and ran down the stairs. Surely my mother would protect me this time I hoped, for I knew this was not a normal outburst. The hatred in his eyes made them bulge. I knew his control had gone; he wanted to hurt me and hurt me badly. He came faster than I thought possible, slipping on the last stair, which intensified his anger. One more stride and his arm swung out and caught me. His fist seized my shoulder-length hair; my body went rigid with pain as he swung me in the air and I felt strands of hair loosen as they came out of my scalp. I screamed, and then felt my breath leave my body as he threw me face up on the floor. He was still shouting, flecks of spittle forming in the corners of his mouth and dropping onto my face. I saw red eyes, now glazed with fury, felt his hands go round my throat, and knew he wanted to squeeze the life out of me.

The weight of his knee pressed into my stomach, then one hand left my neck, while the other kept up the pressure, and came down time and again on my body. The punches rained down on my breasts and stomach while the words, 'You need a lesson taught to you my girl,' became a chant that he repeated time and time again.

Stars floated in front of my eyes, then I heard my mother's voice raised in a mixture of fear and anger.

'Paddy, get off her.'

The cloud lifted from his eyes and the pressure round my throat eased. Dazed and choking, I took in the scene; saw my mother white faced, her eyes dark with anger, holding the bread knife firmly in her hand. She pointed it at him and repeated her command until his eyes focused on the blade. For a moment he went completely still, allowing me a few seconds to crawl away.

Hope came fleetingly to me. Surely she would do what I had heard her threaten him with in their many rows – leave him and take me with her? Or, even better, tell him to go. Then hope died once more. Instead of hearing what I hoped for I heard words I was too numb to comprehend.

'Get out, Antoinette!' she shouted.

Still I crouched, in the belief that if I didn't move I would be invisible to them. Seeing me not moving, she dragged me by the arm with all the force she could muster, opened the door and with one push threw me out into the street.

'Don't come back tonight,' were her final words before the door closed firmly in my face. I stood outside, my body aching from the force of his blows, shivering both from fear and the chill of the evening. Shock and fright paralysed me for a few seconds and I felt a helpless panic. Where was I to go? I knew better than to seek help from one of the family. If I did I would receive a worse punishment on my return. He was the son, the brother, the nephew, who could do no wrong and I would be seen as a liar, a troublemaker, who would not be believed. They would simply bring me back. This I knew as I paused for those few seconds until fear lent my feet wings and I took off into the night.

I went to the flat which Isabel, one of our teachers, shared with a friend. I told them through hiccups and tears that I had had a terrible row with my parents for leaving my bedroom untidy and I was scared to go home. They were sympathetic; they were only recently qualified teachers and knew how dictatorial Irish fathers could be. Their efforts of reassuring me that it would all blow over, and that really my parents must be worried about me, only brought on a fresh bout of tears. They phoned my mother to tell her where I was. She, they told me, was not angry, just relieved that I was safe, but as it was so late she gave her permission for me to stay there. My father had gone to work, she told them, upset by both my behaviour and my disappearance. He thought I had gone to my grandparents' house and would therefore be all right. I was at that age when I showed him no respect. I was to go straight home in the morning, when she would deal with me, and of course I would go to school as normal. She apologized for the inconvenience, telling them that I caused nothing but trouble at home, giving her constant worry and sleepless nights.

If they were surprised that a child known for her good behaviour during school hours could be so disruptive out of them, they passed no comment. A bed was made up for me on the settee and I quickly fell into a deep sleep. In the morning they lent me the bus fare for the return journey home. Remembering that they were responsible adults and I not much more than a child, instructions to behave followed me as, with a sinking feeling of dread, I left the safety of their flat and made my way to the bus stop.

My father had returned from his nightshift and was already in bed when I arrived home and knocked on the door. My mother silently let me in, a reproving look on her face, and then put my breakfast out. She told me she'd slept badly because of me; then asked me to make more of an effort to get on with my father.

'I can't take much more,' she said. 'I'm tired of you worrying me; tired of you doing things that upset him.'

Underneath the surface I thought I could sense her fear; my father had gone too far that night. It was only her intervention that had stopped a potential scandal even worse than what was to follow.

Although he had never in all the years he had beaten me laid a finger on her she must have finally become aware of what he was capable of. That was the only time she mentioned the events of that evening and in the afternoon I came home to find my father waiting for me.

'I'm going to tell,' I said weakly as I tried to stand up to him. 'I'm going to tell if you hit me again.'

He laughed at me; a laugh that had no hint of fear in it, then very calmly replied, 'Antoinette, nobody will believe you. You talk my girl and it's you who'll be sorry. Everyone will blame you. You've kept quiet, haven't you? You've kept quiet for years.'

My silence was enough to allow him to continue with a note of triumph in his voice.

'So, you're just as guilty as me. Your family won't love you anymore. If you bring disgrace to this house your mother won't want you. You'll be the one sent away, you'll be put into a home and you'll never see your mother again. You'll go to strangers; strangers who'll know how bad you are. Is that what you want? Is it?'

I saw in my mind's eye a picture of angry people sneering at me, and felt the bleakness of an unfamiliar world without my mother.

'No,' I whispered, scared of the future he'd just shown me. I'd heard stories of how people were treated in the homes once their parents had handed them over. Knowing he'd won again, he smirked.

'So, if you don't want more of what you got last night you just behave. Now get out of my sight. Get upstairs till I've gone. I've done with you.'

I did as he commanded.

'And don't be leaving your bedroom untidy, do you hear me Antoinette?' His voice continued to mock me from the bottom of the stairs, and I sat on the edge of my bed till his breathing told me he'd gone to sleep.

Chapter Twenty-One

Gripped by inertia, feeling as if my inner strength had abandoned me since my beating, I tried to avoid my parents as much as possible. I had my Saturday job and my visits to my grandparents, which he could not deny me. But requests to see my friends in Portrush were now frequently refused, and the rides on my bicycle, which had always calmed me in the past, were now strictly monitored. A strange atmosphere pervaded the house and my father's unpredictable temper, which had so often turned to rage, seemed to have transformed into something even darker. Often I could feel his gaze on me, partly an expression that I knew, but behind it another unfamiliar one lurked, filling me with fear.

One day, when I had been on the school summer holidays for a week, my mother was getting ready to leave for work. I knew my father had returned to the house earlier and was in bed. From my bedroom, just across the landing from theirs, I'd heard him first enter the bathroom, urinate without closing the door, and then pad noisily back into their bedroom. When I heard the click of the door closing, which announced my mother's departure, I crept downstairs. As quietly as I could I lit the stove to boil water for my morning wash and tea, then lit the grill to make myself a slice of toast. Then his voice roared down the stairs.

'Antoinette, get yourself up here.'

I felt panic rise in me as I went up, standing mutely at his door.

'Make me some tea and bring it up.'

I turned to go. 'I've not finished with you yet my girl.'

A lump rose in my throat, threatening to choke me, making words impossible as I turned to look at him and met his mocking gaze. He smiled humourlessly at me.

'You can bring me some toast as well.'

Robot-like, I made his tea and toast. Placing it on a tray I carried it up to him. Pushing aside the overflowing ashtray and packet of cigarettes, I placed the tray on the small bedside table and prayed that was all he wanted, knowing it wasn't going to be.

Out of the corner of my eye I saw with a feeling of revulsion his pale freckled chest, the now greying hair poking out above his grubby vest, and smelt his sour body odour, which mingled with the stale smell of tobacco that lingered in the room. Then I felt his excitement.

'Take your clothes off, Antoinette. I've a present for you. Take them all off, and do it slowly.'

I turned to look at him. He'd never asked for that before. His eyes mocked and defiled me.

'Antoinette, I'm speaking to you, take them off here,' he repeated between noisy slurps of tea.

Suddenly he was out of bed, clad only in his grubby vest with his erection standing out from under the fold of his paunchy stomach. Seeing I was reluctantly doing as he told me he smiled, came closer to me and gave me a stinging slap across my buttocks.

'Hurry up now,' he whispered.

Still holding my gaze, while I stood like a rabbit caught in the glare of sudden light, my clothes in a heap on the floor, feeling an overwhelming urge to run but having neither the willpower nor a place to run to, he picked up his jacket, taking a small packet out of his pocket, just like all the others I had seen before. He opened it, took out the small balloon-like object and eased it over his swollen member. For a few seconds he grasped my hand, holding it as he eased the condom on, then forcing my unyielding fingers to move up and down until it was firmly in place.

Suddenly he released me, took my shoulders in a firm grasp and threw me on the bed with so much violence that it caused the mattress to bounce and squeak on its old spiral springs. He seized my legs, pulled them apart and high and entered me with a force that ripped into my body and penetrated the whole of my inside with a searing pain. The muscles of my inner thighs stretched as again and again he plunged into me. His calloused hands grasped my breasts, which of late had become uncomfortably sore, twisting my nipples with an anger that fuelled his excitement as he slobbered over my face and neck. I felt the bristles of his unshaven chin scrape my skin. I bit my lip to stop myself from giving him the satisfaction I knew he wanted of hearing me cry out. My whole body shook with his heaving as I clenched my fists, which lay by my side, and squeezed my eyes tightly shut to keep my tears in. His body shuddered as he reached satisfaction, and with a grunt he rolled off me.

Hurriedly I sat up. As I bent over to pick up my clothes I saw his shrivelled penis; hanging from the end was the small grey-white blob of rubber. The lump in my throat rose and as I rushed to the toilet it turned into hot bile, burning my throat as it gushed in a torrent into the toilet. When I felt there was nothing left in my body to come up, and not wanting to wait for the saucepan to boil, I filled the basin with cold water.

Looking in the mirror I saw a pale face, with tear-filled eyes and red blotches on her chin and neck, staring despairingly back at me. Again and again I washed myself, but still his smell lingered on me until I believed it had become a permanent stain on my body.

The sound of his contented snores resounded from my parents' room as I went downstairs, thinking that at least he would sleep for several hours, allowing me to make an escape from the house.

Opening the front door to the fresh air, I let Judy out. Sitting on the grass I put my arms around her neck, laid my cheek against her head and let my tears flow. Judy, sensing my despair, gave my face warm licks to show her love. It felt so unlike my father's slobbering.

'When,' I asked myself hopelessly, 'will this end?'

Unable to bear being anywhere near him, I took my bike, which only a short time before had filled me with such a sense of achievement when I had purchased it with my own money, and listlessly peddled away.

I cycled aimlessly, until fields replaced the streets of houses. Twice I had to dismount, leaving my bike by the verge as the bile rose in my throat again, causing me to retch and retch until the tears streamed down my face, even after the thin stream of yellow bile had dried up.

I sat in a field part of that day, a blank in my head where my mind should have been, until finally I wearily cycled home to attend to the household chores before my mother returned from work.

Chapter Twenty-Two

I was certain I was ill. Nausea seemed to have me in its grip every waking hour. On rising I would rush to the toilet, and vomit until there was nothing left inside me. During the nights my hair grew lank, soaked in perspiration from my head and neck. Beads of moisture would form on my forehead and upper lip whilst my whole body felt cold. There was a fear inside me, a feeling of impending doom as daily my body felt heavier and weaker. My breasts felt sore to touch, my stomach was rejecting food but appearing to swell from the lack of it. The waistband of my new trousers now dug into me, causing red welts to appear on my fair skin.

My mother's anger became a constant, palpable presence whenever I was around her, while my father's eyes seemed to follow my every move. In the evenings, when he was at work, an uneasy silence would descend until my mother finally admitted she knew I was ill.

'Antoinette,' she said as I sat trying to read,'take yourself to the doctor tomorrow.'

I looked up at her, hoping to see some concern, but I only saw an expressionless face, while in her eyes lurked an emotion I couldn't name.

In the late 1950s, a phone call to a doctor's surgery gained an instant appointment. My early morning call resulted in me waiting nervously in his waiting room at eleven o'clock. The nurse who ushered me in gave me a friendly smile, which when I left less than half an hour later had been replaced by a look of cold disdain.

The doctor on duty that day was not the elderly man I had met on several previous occasions, but a handsome young man with floppy blond hair and startling blue eyes. Introducing himself as a locum who was filling in for the family practitioner, he waved me towards a chair placed opposite him. A dark wood desk separated us, bare except for my slim medical file, which he opened, then glanced quickly inside.

'What has brought you here today, Antoinette?' he asked, as he gave me a bland, professional smile. The smile slowly left his face as I told him my symptoms. He asked me about my periods, when the last one had been and I tried to remember when I had asked my mother for sanitary towels. I had felt too ill to realize that three months had passed, nor would I have seen the importance of it.

'Do you think you could be pregnant?' was his next question.

'No,' I replied, without a moment's hesitation.

The years had taught me how to gauge adults' reactions, and underneath his professional manner I sensed something adverse as I shifted from being a teenage patient to someone he saw as a potential problem.

He told me to go behind the screen, undress from the waist down and cover myself with the sheet provided. As I did what he had asked I heard him call for his nurse to come in.

I lay, staring at the ceiling with my knees both raised and apart while he prodded inside me with his latex-gloved hand. A few minutes later he told me to dress. He drew off his glove and I heard him throw it into the bin. I noticed the look exchanged between the nurse and him as he quietly dismissed her.

For the second time he motioned me to sit but now his face was wearing a stern expression.

'Do you know the facts of life?' he asked, his voice cold.

Dismally, knowing what he was going to say next but still not accepting it, I answered. 'Yes.'

'You are three months pregnant,' was all I heard through the clouds of my despair.

'I can't be, I've never slept with a boy,' I blurted out in denial of what I knew to be true.

'You must have slept with one,' he retorted, impatient with what he perceived to be an obvious lie.

I gazed at him, hoping to see some hint of help but finding only the judgement he had now come to about me reflected in his eyes.

'Only with my father,' I finally replied.

A frozen silence descended on the room as the words of my secret hung in the air, spoken aloud for the first time ever.

'Did he rape you?' he asked with a sudden note of sympathy in his voice.

Hearing even a hint of kindness brought tears to my eyes. I mumbled through them, 'Yes.'

'Does your mother know?'

Now the tears were flowing but I managed to shake my head and mutter, 'No.'

'You must ask her to ring me,' he told me as he passed some tissues over the desk. 'I will have to talk to her.'

I was shaking as I rose on trembling legs and left the surgery. Outside, terror paralysed me. Where could I go? I wondered, not home. How could I go home? He was there. Through my terror a face floated into my mind, that of Isabel, my teacher who had given me sanctuary after the beating. She had left the school at the beginning of the summer holidays to get married but I knew she was back from her honeymoon now. She had helped me once – surely she would help me again?

Hurriedly I rode my bicycle to the nearest telephone box, where I found her new husband's name and address in the directory. Not stopping to ring her, just praying that she would be at home, I cycled to the address.

Entering one of the new housing estates, which had sprung up over the previous few years, I quickly found where she lived. It was an imposing mock-Georgian house. I dismounted and leant my bicycle against the wall.

'She will help me,' I told myself. 'She will let me stay here. She won't send me back.' The words were going through my mind like a mantra as I walked up the newly laid path, flanked either side by black soil scattered with the green dots of freshly sown grass.

Isabel opened the door to me with a surprised but not unwelcoming look, and I felt the tears that any show of kindness brought trickle unchecked down my cheeks. Quickly she ushered me inside and sat me down on an orange settee in her freshly painted brown and cream living room.

'Antoinette, what's wrong?' she asked gently as she passed me a clean white handkerchief.

I trusted in her, so I told her what the doctor had said. I explained why I was so scared, and how ill I felt. The same silence that had hung in the doctor's room now hung in her front room, and on her face I saw her look of concern had been replaced by fright.

'Antoinette,' she said, 'stay here. My husband's home for his lunch – he's in the kitchen. Just give me a few minutes will you?'

With that she left the room and only the ticking of a clock, which sat on the mantelpiece of a stone fireplace, broke the silence as I sat waiting for her return.

But she didn't return, instead her husband entered the room. I knew from his grim, unsmiling expression that there was going to be no refuge in their home for me.

'Is it true, what you've just told my wife?' were his opening words.

All confidence left me and I could only miserably nod my head and whisper, 'Yes.'

Taking no notice of my discomfort he continued: 'Well, she's very upset. She's pregnant and I can't have her distressed. I don't know what purpose you thought would be served by your coming here, but you have to go home and talk to your mother.'

He walked to the door, motioning me to follow. Wordlessly I did as he instructed, and then looked at him once more, hoping for some reprieve. There was none.

'My wife does not want to see you here again,' were his last words as he closed the door with a finality that over the next weeks I would come to expect from everyone, even though I couldn't understand it.

I heard my father's warning echoing in my ears. 'Everyone will blame you. Your mother won't love you if you talk.'

I picked up my bicycle and rode home. My father was in bed when I returned, but not asleep.

'Antoinette,' he called out as soon as I was through the door, 'come up here.'

Feeling heavy with foreboding I climbed the stairs to face him.

'What did the doctor say?' he asked, and I knew when I looked into his eyes that he already knew the answer.

'I'm pregnant,' I replied boldly.

For once his face betrayed little of his feelings; he simply pulled the bedclothes up to invite me in.

'I'll get rid of it for you Antoinette. Come on over here

now,' but this time I just stood there and shook my head. My usual terror subsided and a new rage rose as I answered him.

'You did not get rid of it did you, when you put that thing into me? I'm three months pregnant. How many times did you make me do it over that time?'

Satisfaction fleetingly passed by as I saw that the fear which had momentarily left me had taken root in him.

'Did you tell the doctor it was me?' was his next question.

'No,' I lied, the fear returning.

'Well, remember what I've told you my girl, you will be blamed if you talk. You'll be taken away and locked up. Your mother won't stop them. Everyone will blame you.'

I had already seen in three people's faces that what he was predicting was true.

'Now, I'm going to tell your mother that you've told me you went to Portrush, met some English boys and did it with them. Do you hear me, Antoinette? So what are you going to tell your mother?'

The strength left me and I answered as he wanted me to. 'I'm going to tell her that I went with an English boy and he's gone now.'

He told me to go to my room and wait there until he'd spoken to her. Meekly, I did as he instructed.

After what seemed like hours to me the sound of the front door opening announced her arrival. From my bedroom I could hear the murmur of their voices, although the words were indistinct, then I heard the sound of my father's departure. Still I sat waiting, with my hand on the bulge of my stomach, wanting an adult to sort my problem out, but with no clear idea of how I expected them to do it.

I knew not to leave my room until summoned. Hunger gnawed at my insides. I felt faint and sick, but still I waited until my mother was ready to talk to me.

I heard the whistle of the kettle. Her voice called out for me to go to her. Fearfully, I obeyed. She had poured both of us out cups of tea. Gratefully I picked mine up, held it to my lips and sipped. The hot cup gave my shaking hands something to hold and the sweet liquid calmed me. I felt her stare burning into me, but I refused to return her gaze. Instead I stared into my cup and waited for her to speak, which finally she did.

'Who is the father?' she asked in a cold flat voice. I looked at her and knew my lies would be of no avail, but still I tried. She did not even allow me to finish them.

'Antoinette,' she commanded, 'tell me what the truth is. Tell me and I won't be angry.'

I met her eyes, which held an expression I still could not fathom.

'Daddy,' was all I could choke out.

To which she replied, 'I know.'

Still she stared at me with those large green eyes of hers and I knew that her will power, far stronger than mine, would drag every grain of truth from me. She asked me when it had started, and I told her at the thatched house. I told her about the 'drives' but I still saw little expression on her face.

'All those years,' was her only comment.

She didn't ask me why I'd kept quiet, or why I'd colluded with my father to lie to her. Months later I would remember that and form my own opinion on why.

'Does the doctor know?' she asked.

'Yes,' I replied, and told her that he wanted to see her.

Little did I know that the lie I told when she asked her final question would nearly cost me my life. She asked me if I had told anyone else and I suppressed the painful memory of telling Isabel and replied, 'No.'

I saw a look of relief cross her face as she rose from her chair to reach for the phone. After speaking into it briefly she turned to me.

'I've made an appointment to see the doctor after his surgery. You stay here.' With those parting words she donned her coat and left.

For what seemed an eternity I sat trancelike on a chair, only moving to throw more coal onto the fire or to scratch Judy's head. She, sensing my absolute despair, did not leave my side that evening as I waited for my mother's return and for some answer about what my fate was to be.

The click of the front door opening alerted me to my mother's return, and I looked up to see not one person but two. The doctor had returned with her. Over the next hour they were my judge and jury, and my sentence was silence. My father would be admitted for a short time to hospital to recover from a 'breakdown', a legal abortion would be arranged for me, and then I would, on the doctor's recommendation, be placed in a home for difficult teenagers. There I would stay until school leaving age, when suitable work would be found for me. It would be impossible for my father and I to live under the same roof. Meanwhile, until the abortion was arranged, life would carry on as normal. This was all told to me by my mother, with the silent support of the doctor who, she informed me, had told her it was her only option. Exhausted and uncomprehending I listened to their plans to end the only life that I knew.

Then the doctor spoke to me directly.

'I'm only helping you because of your mother – she's the innocent victim in all of this. You lied to me this morning. You led me to believe it had only happened once.' He paused and gave me a look of cold disdain. 'You encouraged it by keeping quiet for all those years, so don't tell me you're innocent.'

Then he left, leaving my mother and I facing each other. I waited for some word of understanding from her but none came, and not being able to stand the cold silence any longer, still without having eaten, I went to bed.

The next few days passed in a blur. Interviews were arranged at two homes, through which I sat silently, now labelled as a difficult teenager, fourteen years old and pregnant by someone whose name I could not admit to knowing.

Following that came my mini-courtroom hearing where stern-faced men of the medical profession interviewed me in order to determine both the fate of my unborn child and myself. On the grounds of mental instability, it was arranged for the abortion to take place at a hospital in the next town to us, as a concession to try and keep it quiet. Northern Ireland in the late fifties was anti-abortion; nurses and doctors dedicated to saving lives strongly objected to being instructed by a medical court to terminate one, as I was soon to find out.

My parents, united by their bond of complicity, ignored me that week as I waited for the day I was due to have my 'operation' as my mother now referred to it. On the day that my body was to be cleaned out of the proof of my father's guilt, my mother went to work, and I, holding a small overnight case, caught the bus to the hospital.

An unsmiling ward sister showed me to a side ward where my bed and locker were. I knew without asking why they had put me there. I was in the maternity ward and the hospital wanted privacy for the operation that was to be performed on me. At eight o'clock the following morning the sister came to my bedside.

'Have to get you ready,' she said as she placed a bowl of water beside my bed with a razor next to it. 'Undress from the waist down.'

To my humiliation she quickly shaved the tender skin between my legs, roughly dragging the razor across it, leaving small nicks in my skin. During all the time she was there, those were the only words she spoke to me. When she had finished she silently picked up the bowl and razor and left.

Her next visit to my bedside was to hastily inject the

premed fluid into my buttocks, leaving me to doze and think. I wanted my mother; I wanted someone to tell me I was going to be all right. I wanted to know what was going to be done to me, because no one had told me anything. Most of all I wanted someone to hold my hand. I was so scared. Then, mercifully, I fell asleep.

In my half-asleep stupor I felt hands on me, heard a voice saying, 'Come on Antoinette, move on to the trolley now,' and I felt myself being gently rolled over. A blanket was tucked around me and I felt the movement of the trolley as it was gently pushed. Then it stopped and a bright light penetrated my eyelids. Something covered my nose and a voice told me to count backwards, but I know as consciousness slipped away I called for my mother …

Nausea more intense than I had ever felt interrupted my sleep. Opening my eyes I saw that a metal dish had been placed on my locker. I reached for it to vomit as unheeded tears ran down my face. For a few seconds I wondered where I was. Then I remembered and reached down between my legs to find a sanitary towel had been placed there. Ill informed as I was on the facts of life, I knew the baby had gone.

Sleep returned until the sister came with a tray of tea and sandwiches. As she placed it on my locker I noticed that a clean bowl had replaced the earlier one and wondered how long I had been asleep for.

'Your tea, Antoinette,' she informed me, unnecessarily, as she turned to walk out of the room. Then she glanced back at me with a look of intense dislike. 'Oh, you'd be wanting to know: the baby, it was a boy.'

Then she left and the baby became real to me. I lay there with my appetite gone and grieved for my dead baby boy until sleep returned, taking me into an uneasy slumber where I dreamt again that I was falling.

Morning came and, with the first rays of sun, a ward orderly arrived bearing a tray of tea, toast and a boiled egg. This time, feeling ravenous, I fell upon it, hardly leaving a crumb on the plate. Soon after breakfast the ward sister appeared. Glancing at my empty plate she sniffed disapprovingly, 'See your appetite's all right', then grudgingly she informed me that after the doctor's rounds I would be free to go.

'Is anyone collecting you?' was her only question, and her only response to my answer of 'No', was a small grim smile.

Feeling sticky and dirty I asked her where I could bath and wash my hair.

'The nurse will bring you water to wash. You can bath when you return home. Your hair can wait; sure it's only vanity.' She paused, looking at me with the same expression of cold dislike. 'If it wasn't for vanity, maybe you would not have been in here.' And with that she walked away.

My stomach ached, but I was not going to ask for anything more. Instead I washed as best as I could in the small dish of water that was provided, dressed and waited for the doctor who had performed the operation to arrive.

When he, accompanied by the ward sister, came he hardly

looked at me and didn't ask me how I felt. He simply informed me I was free to leave. So, picking up my case, I walked out of the hospital and went to the bus stop.

Chapter Twenty-Three

Something had woken me, but outside the small window of my bedroom was only darkness, inside only quiet, and for a few seconds I wondered what had disturbed me. My mind struggled to waken as it told my body it must. Then I felt it, a warm stickiness between my legs. My hand crept to my pyjama bottoms and came away warm and wet. Panic rose in me as I swung my legs out over the edge of my metal bed onto the linoleum covered floor and stumbled to the light switch.

The yellow glow from the low-voltage bulb, which hung unadorned by a shade, gleamed dully onto my bed. A puddle of dark red blood stained the sheet. Uncomprehending, I looked down at my pyjamas to see that they were soaked with it. Blood clung to my fingers where I'd touched myself; I could feel it running down my legs as I screamed for my mother.

Within seconds she came, took in at a glance what was wrong with me and instructed me to return to bed. Then my father appeared, bleary eyed in his crumpled pyjamas.

'What's wrong? What's all the noise about?' he muttered.

With a look of disgust my mother pointed to me.

'You'll have to call an ambulance,' he told her and I heard a note of fear in his voice.

'I'll call the doctor,' she replied. 'He'll know what to do.'

Dimly, as though from far away, I heard my mother descend the stairs, heard her voice as she spoke on the phone. Then a few minutes later I heard the voice of the doctor as if through a fog. Opening my eyes, I saw his blurred outline.

As if in a dream their whispered conversation penetrated my ears and drifted into my mind.

'It's bad,' I heard him say. 'She has to go to a hospital. It's up to you, Ruth, which one. The one in town or the one where she had the operation?'

Clearly through my haze I felt the silence, then I heard my mother say, 'The one where she had the operation.'

Then the voices left and I felt myself floating in limbo land, neither awake nor asleep but aware of movement around me. I heard my mother tell my father to stay in their bedroom, heard the doctor's voice talking to her outside my bedroom door, and I knew without caring that I was dying.

A piercing noise, which I recognized as the siren of an ambulance, penetrated the fog I was in and through my window I saw the blue light flashing. Hands lifted me gently. I felt the bump of each stair as the stretcher was carried downstairs, felt it being slid into the ambulance, then heard the siren restart as we drove away.

The picture of my mother, with the doctor, as they stood

side by side outside, watching the door close once I was placed inside, has remained engraved on the retina of my eyes for ever.

The hospital my mother had chosen for me was thirteen miles away. The only roads to it were narrow and winding, as there were no motorways near Coleraine in the late fifties.

I felt cold, icy cold, although the sweat was running from my body, and the blood seeped out between my legs. Black spots danced in front of my eyes while a bell started to ring in my ears, almost obliterating the noise of the siren.

A hand stroked my head, then reached for my hand as a spasm shook my body, and bile drooled from my mouth.

'She's going! Drive faster, man,' I heard a voice shout. The ambulance shuddered with the driver's efforts and I heard the walkie-talkie radio crackle into life as instructions were shouted into it.

'Hold on, Antoinette, don't go to sleep now', the same voice pleaded with me above the ringing in my ears, then I felt a bump as we screeched to a halt. I felt the stretcher being lifted, heard running footsteps as unseen bodies carried it, then bright lights dazzled me. There was a stinging sensation in my arm and my eyes stopped trying to focus on the white-coated bodies that surrounded me.

A figure in blue was at my bedside when next I awoke. My eyes met the brown ones of the ward sister. Her hostility had disappeared and compassion had replaced it, now I was a patient in need of her care. Gently she stroked my head, held the bowl as I vomited into it, then sponged my face with a cool, damp cloth.

At the side of my bed, I could see a clear plastic bag suspended on a metal pole; inside it was a red fluid, which I knew to be blood. A tube led from the bag to my arm where a needle was taped on to it.

'Why, Antoinette, did they send you back here?' she was asking, unbelievingly. 'Why not to the nearest hospital?' I had a feeling she knew the reason as well as I did.

Not answering her I closed my eyes, but in my mind's eye I kept seeing the image of my mother watching me being lifted into the ambulance as I went on what she must have believed to be my final journey. Not wanting to accept what I knew to be true, I forced that memory into a box, one I never opened.

'Stop,' I silently screamed in the hospice as I tried to shut out the whisper of that childish voice. 'Stop. I want the lid of that memory box left closed!'

'No, Toni, you have to remember it all,' the soft voice murmured firmly as I felt myself being pulled between two worlds: the one where Antoinette lived and the one I had created. Against my wishes my inherited game of 'being a member of a happy family' was being forced to an end.

The box stayed open and I saw again the picture of my mother standing next to the doctor outside the ambulance as my stretcher was placed inside.

The next time I awoke the sister was again sitting at my side.

'Am I going to die?' I heard myself ask.

She lent across, took my hand and gently squeezed it. I saw a gleam of moisture film her eyes. 'No, Antoinette, you gave us a fright but you will be all right now.' She then tucked the bedclothes around me and I fell into a deep sleep.

Two more days passed in the hospital. Doctors came, said soothing words and left. In my waking hours I lay gazing hopefully at the door as I waited for the mother I still loved to come, until the bitter realization dawned on me that she was never going to.

Tempting food was brought to me in vain. Feeling depressed and unwanted, I just pushed it around the plate and left most of it uneaten. On the third day the sister once again sat by my bedside, took my hand and gently stroked it.

'Antoinette, you can go home today.' She paused, and I knew that more was to come. 'You should never have had that operation – you were too many months along.' I heard anger in her voice that for the first time was not directed at me. 'Antoinette, you almost died. The doctors had to work hard to save you, but I have to tell you something.' Still I waited as she struggled to find the right words to tell me something that she knew I would find devastating. 'Oh child, whatever you did you don't deserve this. Antoinette, you will never be able to have children.'

I gazed at her uncomprehendingly at first, and then her words sunk in. As my hope of one day having someone to love me, having a family of my own to care for, left me, I turned my face away to hide the feeling of absolute emptiness that swamped me.

Later that morning she returned.

'Come Antoinette, let's get you into a bath before you go home,' she said with a cheerfulness I was aware she did not feel. Somehow I knew there was still something she had not told me, but listlessness dampened my curiosity and I followed her wordlessly.

In the bath I washed my hair and tried to scrub away the memories that soiled me, then reluctantly I climbed out, towel dried myself and put on my clothes, which now hung loosely on my thinner frame.

A bag had been delivered for me that must have been packed by my mother, containing my trousers, shirt, toiletries and a small amount of money. The doctor had brought it in I was told when I enquired.

Feeling that I had been completely abandoned, I packed my few possessions, and on legs that still felt weak I walked out of the hospital to the bus stop where I caught the first of the two buses I needed to get me home. Sitting outside was my father's Jaguar, which told me he was in. Parked beside it was a car I did not recognize.

Nervously I opened the door. My parents were waiting for me with the doctor. The doctor spoke first.

'Your friend the teacher has gone to social services. They have informed the police – they are coming in the next few minutes.'

After those words he left and silence descended. I felt ill and weak, my stomach ached and my head started pounding with the build-up of pressure. We all heard the car pull up outside and my mother raised herself from the chair and, stony faced, went to let the police in.

'In future,' she said as they walked in, 'if you need to speak to my husband or daughter, would you have the decency to come in an unmarked car? I've done nothing wrong and I refuse to be embarrassed.'

The policeman who introduced himself as the sergeant in charge of the case gave her an inscrutable look, simply read my father his rights and then requested both of us to accompany him and his female constable to the police station. He asked my mother, as I was a minor, if she wanted to be present when I was interviewed. She declined the offer. She was then informed that a social worker would be present in her place.

My father and I were escorted to the car and we all drove off. I knew that although one nightmare had ended, another one had started. But I had no way of knowing how terrible it would be.

Chapter Twenty-Four

Thirteen days had passed since I arrived at the hospice. Now the clatter of the breakfast trolley no longer heralded my release, because now I had a new painstaking duty. Spoonful by spoonful I would have to feed my mother. First I placed a napkin around her neck, then held a cup to her lips to allow her to sip her morning tea. She would sit with her hands folded. Her eyes, now dull, looked into mine as our circle of role reversal was completed. Small portions of lightly scrambled eggs or smooth fruity yoghurts would then need to be spooned into her mouth. After each mouthful I would gently wipe around her lips with a damp cloth as the residue trickled down her chin.

Doctors' rounds followed the departure of the trolleys. 'How long?' I would silently ask, but their faces gave nothing away.

It was my father's visit that now I waited for. At the sound of his tread I would rise and make my way to the lounge where coffee and cigarettes awaited me. The solitude of the lounge was not to be that day, for another woman sat in the area for smokers with an unopened book lying on her knee.

Tentatively she smiled, then introduced herself as Jane. Over the next hour we learnt that both of us were sleeping at the hospice. For her these were the last days of what had been a happy marriage and her final gift of love to her husband. His bone cancer, she informed me, had now spread to his brain and he hardly recognized her. The loss that was to come had etched fine lines upon her face and smudged dark shadows under her eyes.

I silently applauded her courage; she was looking at the end of her life as she knew it, whereas I had mine to return to.

Our conversation drifted to asking the questions which form the first steps of forging a friendship, even though we both knew it would only be a temporary one. She asked me my surname and where I came from in Ireland. Without thinking I told her.

'Why, Coleraine is my home town,' she exclaimed as, with momentary pleasure, she discovered a bond between us. 'You have a familiar look about you – have you a cousin called Maddy?'

Memories of my Irish family and my numerous relatives, unseen for many years, sprung into my mind as, for a few seconds, I returned to Coleraine. As I searched for the right words I saw fleeting expressions of recognition and embarrassment cross her face. Knowing that in a hospice friendships are just ships that pass in the night, formed to give support through difficult and painful days and nights, I felt no awkwardness. Instead I simply answered her.

'She's my father's cousin.'

Her gaze focused on a spot above my shoulder and without either hearing or seeing him I felt my father's presence. Feeling incapable of any other choice I hurriedly introduced them.

To his 'hallo' and questioning look, she filled in the silence with a forced brightness I was sure she did not feel.

'Yes, your daughter and I were just having a conversation about Coleraine – that's where we come from too.'

The silence that followed her innocent remark hung heavily in the air, then my father managed to find a polite response.

'Nice meeting you. Excuse me, but I have to speak to my daughter now.'

I felt his fingers close on my elbow. He propelled me to the corner furthest from Jane, and then abruptly let me go. I looked into his face, into those glowering bloodshot eyes of his, and saw that all trace of the sad old man from a few days ago had disappeared. In his place was the 'nasty' father of my childhood. I saw not the man fast approaching eighty but the angry forty-year-old the year he went to prison. The years fell away, taking my adult self with them, leaving in their wake that small, frightened child who once had been me.

Through my inherent fear I heard his threatening voice: 'Don't you be talking about our business, my girl. There's no call for you to be saying that you lived in Coleraine. Don't you be telling what school you went to. Do you hear me now, Antoinette?'

The six-year-old that lived inside me nodded her head and whispered, 'Yes.'

My adult self knew that the moment for subterfuge had passed. My parents' fear of being recognized if they stepped outside their insular lives had now been realized. How ironic, I thought, that it was my mother's fear of dying that had made it a reality.

I fought for control over both the fear and the hatred from my childhood, forcing the mask of Toni, the successful businesswoman, back onto my face. Giving him a look of contempt, I walked away.

On returning to my mother's ward I saw a fresh vase of flowers proudly displayed by her bedside. Smiling with the animation that my father's visits often brought her, she pointed to them. 'Look, dear, what Daddy's brought.'

Let the game of happy families begin, I thought wearily, but the feel of his fingers on my arm stayed imprinted on my mind as I slipped into the role of dutiful daughter.

The afternoon routine no longer included the slow, agonizing shuffle to the bathroom. Tubes and a plastic bag had replaced that need. Instead I helped her into bed, washed her, then piled the pillows high. Exhausted, she would close her eyes and drift to sleep. I would then open a book and try to lose myself in the pages as I waited for the trolleys that brought tea, supper and painkillers. After the last had been administered, finally I could make my escape to the lounge.

In between the trolleys large families would sit around loved ones' beds, but once my father's visit was over only I kept the vigil by her bedside. A musician would visit to play the melodies that both soothed and entertained the patients, and my mother always asked for her favourite tune. 'Ask her to play "Londonderry Air",' was her nightly request. Then the lyre strings would be lovingly plucked, letting the haunting notes float in the air to an audience of four old ladies and me.

As I sat in the lounge on the thirteenth night, I felt tears sliding down my cheeks and angrily brushed them aside. Control over my memories departed as my memory box for the year of 1959 unlocked itself and the contents flooded out. That year one nightmare had ended and another one began.

The two sides of me fought that night for control: the frightened child that lived inside me and the successful woman I'd worked so hard to become. My vision blurred, I felt the familiar sensation of falling, only this time I was awake, my chest constricted and panic turning my breathing into painful rasps. Light was fading, and then I felt a hand on my shoulder, heard a voice ask, 'Toni, are you all right?'

I looked up to see Jane's gentle eyes gazing with concern into mine. No, I thought, I want to cry, I want to be held, I want to be comforted, I want my memories to go away.

'I'm fine,' I replied, brushing away my tears, then curiosity overcame me. 'You know who I am, don't you?'

Her kind eyes held mine as she nodded. She lightly

squeezed my shoulder as she left me to return to her husband's bedside.

Like waves blown in on an angry storm my memories came crashing into me and I feared I might drown. The mask I had hidden the child behind had slipped; no longer was I the person I had worked so hard to become. In the two weeks I had been in the hospice Toni, the self-possessed businesswoman, had gradually slipped away. Antoinette, the frightened child, the obedient puppet of her parents, had begun to retake possession.

I had lost a lot of weight, and when I looked in the mirror Antoinette's eyes, ringed by dark circles, gazed back at me full of fear and panic, feelings that now threatened to swamp me.

Not being able to escape my memories I felt the past draw me back and felt myself wavering on the edge of sanity, the edge I had teetered on twice before. I felt again that temptation to cross it, for on the other side lay safety. It's a safety where all responsibility for our life is taken away as, childlike, we pass it on to others. Then, embryolike, we can curl up and let the days wash over us until the mind becomes a blank space and is freed for ever from its nightmares.

My sleep, sometimes taken at my mother's bedside, sometimes on a put-you-up bed in the doctor's room, was broken by constant nightmares. In them I was helpless because my control was sliding away from me. Warning bells rang in my head as I felt my adult self regressing. I needed help and

I needed it quickly. This was not going to happen to me, not again. I would not, could not, let it.

I went to the minister. He, thinking he was in for some light relief from ministering to the dying, from holding skeletal hands and passing tissues to the recently bereaved, smilingly ushered me into his office. He did not know that this was not going to be his lucky day.

'I need to talk,' I managed to say as I took a seat, and he saw that all signs of the stoic, controlled woman he knew had disappeared. The look of concern on his face showed that he knew he was going to have to deal with something more than a woman losing her mother. For my mother, at eighty, had lived what in most people's opinions would be considered a long life, and I had had over a year to prepare myself for the final outcome of her cancer. That, he soon realized, was not going to be why I needed to talk to him.

He, a man of compassion and humour, was the minister my mother had asked for several times in the middle of the night, before finding she lacked that final courage to confide her fears to him. After all, how could she repent what she still refused to admit? My mother, I now realized, was going to die with her conviction firmly in place; that conviction that she was the victim would remain at the front of her mind and any doubts she had would continue to be tightly suppressed.

Now he was looking at me expectantly as I lit my nicotine prop with hands that trembled. Haltingly, I told him my story, told him that I was reliving the emotions I had felt as a child but mixed with them was a feeling akin to shame; shame that I had allowed their hold over me to remain for so many years. If my mother had orchestrated the game of happy families when I was a child, I as an adult had perpetrated the same myth.

Why, I asked him, had I done that? Why had I invented a past that included loving parents? Why had I pretended to myself and never found the courage to break free?

'Why do you think you couldn't?' he asked, and then let a silence grow, giving me time to think as he waited patiently for my answer.

'I wanted to be like everyone else when they talked about their childhoods,' I replied. 'I wanted to be seen going to Northern Ireland visiting them, and being part of a family.'

'And were you? Did you ever feel part of your family again?'

I thought of the truth then, the things I had tolerated, the things I had accepted and never challenged.

'No, I would always try and visit when my father went to his family. After the day they banned me from their homes I never saw any of them again. My grandparents, aunts, uncles and cousins remained *his* family but ceased to be mine.'

I paused for a moment and admitted what I had not acknowledged even to myself before. 'Do you know, when I was in my teens deep down I missed them so much but I never let myself think about it, never admitted how lonely I was. I've never allowed myself to feel bitterness, but when my grandmother told me that I was no longer welcome in their homes I was numb with despair.'

I paused for a moment as I remembered those feelings of being so rejected.

'What I felt was deeper than loneliness; it was a feeling of being alien to everyone in the world. In later years, when he went to a family wedding, of which there were several, and I was never invited I didn't question it. I accepted the fact that I was not wanted. I never commented on the unfairness of it. I knew that collectively their minds were made up; there was no going back, for they had banished me from their hearts, but not him. I was even excluded from my grandmother's funeral. Once she had loved me and I her. All that was taken away from me by his actions, not mine, and my mother never spoke of it. She just accepted it.'

'What about your relatives in England? You were close to some of them once.'

'The years when my father was in prison, the years I had spent in a mental hospital, left too many gaps for me to have easy conversations with them. I never felt comfortable for they, the few I saw when I first left Northern Ireland, could not understand why I lived away from home and did the jobs I did to survive. They, I think, saw me more as my father's daughter, a man they had always considered their social inferior, and of course I had so much to hide that I must have come across as secretive. I was someone who did not fit in. I could have seen them, I suppose, but I chose not to.'

Even my grandmother, whom I had been so close to when I was in England, had been separated from me by the family secrets. She was not allowed to know why I had left school early and given up the plans for university that I had once described so enthusiastically to her. I only saw her a few more times before she died.

The minister looked at me with sympathy. 'So, as a teenager you had no one, no siblings, no extended family, no aunts and uncles to turn to, only your parents.' Then he shot an unexpected question at me, 'Did you love them?'

'I loved my mother. That never changed. I never loved my father. As a small child he was away so much that he just seemed like a visitor who brought me presents. Oh, he could be immensely charming when he wanted to be, but I was always scared of him. Even now my feelings are mixed. That's what is so confusing. One moment I see this old man who still loves his wife, like he always did. I know how well he looked after her when she became ill, and then I remember the monster of my childhood. He can still intimidate me now,' I finally acknowledged.

'Love is a hard habit to break,' he said gently. 'Ask any woman who has stayed in a bad relationship long after it has ceased to work. Women who have had to flee to refuges so often take their abusive partners back. Why? Because they are in love not with the men who have abused them, but the men they thought they married. They search for that person again and again. Your ties of love were formed when you were a baby: the bond between mother and daughter forged then. If your father had been cruel to her maybe you could have learnt to hate him, but he wasn't and your mother brainwashed you, as well as herself, into the belief that she was a victim of your behaviour. Your emotions are at war with your logic. Emotionally you are carrying your childhood guilt; logically you know that your parents do not deserve you and, certainly, you did not deserve them, no child did. I'm a man of God, I preach forgiveness but, Toni, you have to be clear on the roles your parents played, you have to accept the part your mother participated in, in order to free yourself, for that is the one thing you have never come to terms with.'

His words seemed to lift the barriers with which I had surrounded the truth. The words, once released, seemed to pour out of me in a torrent. I told him how she had constantly said that I must 'get on with my father', how she had 'suffered enough', how she was on 'one dose of medication after another' for her nerves. How I had always 'given her worry'.

'I dreaded phoning home but I did so nearly every week and I knew that her usual refrain would ring in my ears, "Just a moment darling, Daddy wants a word", and over all those years I humoured her, frightened of her love being withdrawn if I made her face reality.'

And finally I told him what I'd never explained to anyone, what I felt about Antoinette, the child who had once been me.

'She would have been so different if she had been allowed to grow up normally, gone to university, made friends. She never stood a chance, and every time something goes wrong in my life I blame that childhood for it. When I was much younger she took over and I relived all of her emotions again. That's when I'd walk into mentally abusive relationships saying, "Hallo, I'm here, this feels like home." Or my old childhood friend, the bottle, would reappear. I've fought those demons all my life and most of the time I've won, but I'm not winning now.'

The ashtray became full as I talked, my head clearing as I accepted the final reality.

'She never loved me. She needs me now so that she can die in peace, with her dream intact; the dream of a good-looking husband who adores her, a happy marriage and one child. I'm just a player in her last act. That's my role here.'

'And are you going to shatter that dream?'

I thought of the tiny form of my mother, so dependent on me now. 'No,' I sighed. 'How could I?'

Chapter Twenty-Five

I'd been placed in a small, airless room in the police station, furnished only with a brown Formica-topped table and a few wooden chairs. Under my feet I could see brown cracked lino and the one small window was set too high in the nicotine-stained wall to afford any outside view. I knew my father was nearby. I knew my nightmare had to have come to an end, but instead of relief I felt apprehension. What would the future hold now, I wondered.

The door opened and I looked round to see the police-woman from earlier, only this time she was accompanied by another young woman dressed in civilian clothes. They asked me if I'd eaten. On the shake of my head the policewoman left to return a few minutes later with a tray holding tea, sand-wiches and some chocolate biscuits, which she placed in front of me with a friendly smile. Notebooks were produced, telling me that however relaxed they were trying to make the atmos-phere, this was official. The woman in civilian clothes was introduced to me as a social worker called Jean and I was asked if I knew why I was there. Then they asked if I was completely aware that what my father and I had done was a crime. To both of those questions I replied in a whisper, 'Yes.'

Gently, the policewoman explained that my father was also being questioned in another room and all I had to do was tell the truth. It was also explained that as I was under age the crime was his and without doubt he would go to prison for it.

'Antoinette, you have done nothing wrong, but we do have to ask you some questions. Are you up to answering them?' the policewoman asked.

I stared at her. How could I find my voice to talk about a secret I had kept for so many years? A secret my father had told me repeatedly I would be blamed for. I had already found out that once discovered it would lead to the anger and blame he had predicted.

Then the social worker spoke for the first time.

'Antoinette, I want to help you, but I can only do that when I have your side of the story. I know this is painful for you but we are on your side.'

She stretched her hand across the desk and gently took my hand. 'Please answer these questions.'

The first one to be taken down for evidence was asked by the policewoman.

'How old were you when your father first touched you?'

I felt the warm pressure of Jean's hand on mine.

'Six,' I finally whispered, and then the tears came. A silent torrent gushed from my eyes and poured down my cheeks. The tissues were passed to me without a word. Neither woman spoke until I had composed myself.

'Why have you kept quiet for all these years? Did you not tell your mother at least?' were the first questions put to me by Jean.

No words came, my memory box stayed shut; the time I had tried to tell my mother stayed firmly locked away as I shook my head. Would my life have been different if I had remembered then and told them? Certainly I would have been taken away from her and events which damaged me later would not have happened. Or would that love for her have always influenced me and affected my life? Even now it's not a question I have found the answer to.

Gently they prised out of me how at weekends he had taken me for drives, how he told me I would be taken away if I talked, how people would blame me and how my mother would cease to love me. On hearing this I saw a look I understood exchanged between the two women. They knew his threats were the truth. They both knew better than me that everything he had threatened and worse was going to come true for me, as I was to learn, and that any remnants of childhood had finally left me.

Gradually my story was drawn from me with sympathetic questions, to which I replied truthfully. But I found it impossible to volunteer any additional information. It would be many years before I would be able to speak about my childhood freely, without shame and guilt. They asked me if I had not been scared of becoming pregnant. I replied that I thought it was impossible to become pregnant by my father.

The ticking of the clock marked the time as it sped away. Tiredness and hopelessness filled me equally as I wondered over and over what was going to happen to me now.

'What are your plans for the future?' the social worker asked. 'Will you be able to stay on at school now?'

Looking at her blankly at first, I suddenly realized what she meant. I was a fee-paying pupil, my father was going to prison and although my mother worked his was the larger wage. Suddenly I was aware of the enormity of what I had done, what harm I had caused; my parents' house was bought on a bank loan, my mother could not drive and my fees could not be paid. All thought of the home my parents had wanted to hide me away in left my mind and a guilty panic replaced it. I had, I realized, ruined my mother's life.

Seeing my blank look turn to one of comprehension as some of what was to face me penetrated my mind, she tried to reassure me.

'Antoinette, this is not your fault. Surely your mother must have guessed over all those years?'

Believing such a thing would have been too much for me to bear. How could I handle the thought of such a betrayal from the one person I loved unconditionally? Desperately I denied it to them, just as I denied it to myself, and again I saw a look exchanged between them, a look that combined pity and disbelief.

'Antoinette,' the policewoman said, her eyes holding a

mixture of compassion and a resolution to do her job, 'you are going to have to be a witness at your father's trial – do you understand what that means?'

Before I had time to digest what that would mean, she added to my fear by informing me that he would be released on bail and both he and I would be returned home together. Then she left the room, leaving me with the social worker. I sat silently while the facts sunk into my mind, then my fear rose unchecked.

'I can't go home,' I stuttered, 'please.'

I felt Jean's pity as she answered. 'Unless the police state that you are at risk there's nothing I can do.'

Long minutes passed before the door opened to admit the policewoman accompanied by her sergeant. Unsmiling, they both sat down to face me.

'Your father has admitted guilt,' the sergeant baldly informed me. 'That makes the trial easier for you. The case will be held *in camera* because you are a minor. Do you know what that means?'

I shook my head as I tried to whisper no.

'That means that no press or members of the public unconnected with the case will be admitted. The trial date has not been decided yet, but it will only be a few weeks away. Now we are going to take both you and your father home.'

I burst into tears. Still feeling weak from my blood loss and emergency operation, all powers of resistance deserted me. I felt paralysed with fear.

'Please don't send me back,' I managed to gasp between

sobs, remembering the beating I'd received for not hanging up my gymslip. If he'd done that for such a small misdemeanour, what punishment would be meted out to me for this? In terror my fingers grasped the edge of the table, as though by clinging on I could postpone the moment I had to go home.

The policewoman was the first to speak. 'We have nowhere to put someone of your age, Antoinette, but your parents won't hurt you again. The sergeant as well as Jean and I are coming with you to speak to your mother.'

The sergeant tried to reassure me further. 'Your father has already been spoken to; he knows the consequences if he touches you again.'

Their words were a cold comfort to me because I could remember my mother's rage, the doctor's disdain and my father's many acts of cruelty. I knew that I was being returned to a home where I was not wanted, to a mother who no longer loved me and a man who would blame me for everything that was now going to happen to the family.

We were driven back in two unmarked cars, as my mother had requested. We drew up to the house where the lights were still on. My mother, unsmiling, let us all in, then mercifully allowed me to disappear upstairs to my room, where the murmur of voices could be heard but not understood. Hunger gnawed at me as I realized that apart from the sandwiches the policewoman had given me, I hadn't eaten since breakfast time in the hospital. I wondered if my mother would think of that, but when I finally heard the door close on the police no footsteps approached my room. Eventually I drifted into a restless sleep in which dreams spread their fear. I woke up to a silent house.

Chapter Twenty-Six

The day I had been looking forward to with dread had come. The day my father was to be tried and sentenced for the crime he had committed against me, the crime of multiple rapes.

My mother, who still protested she was the victim in this triangle, had refused to accompany me to the court. Instead she had gone to work as normal. The sergeant, feeling that I needed female support, had told me he would bring his wife to look after me. Standing at the window at home, too apprehensive to sit, I waited for them to appear.

My father had already left to make his own way to the courtroom, leaving his car behind, which told me that whatever his solicitor had said, he knew he would not be returning home at the end of the day. At least I had been spared his presence that morning.

Unable to relax, I'd been ready since I'd awoken several hours earlier. I'd dressed in a grey skirt and blouse with my school blazer over it. I wondered whether I was still entitled to wear it, but having no other jacket I had no choice.

Judy had had her morning walk. My mainly uneaten breakfast had long ago been finished when the sound of a car's engine announced the arrival of the sergeant. Dressed in his everyday uniform of tweed jacket and grey trousers, he opened the car door for me and introduced his wife, a small plump woman who acknowledged my presence with a small, tight smile. Then we drove the short journey to the courts. Conversation was stilted in the car. All I could see in my mind was my mother's cold stare whenever she had to look at me. Now my wish for a home where only my mother and I would live was finally to come true; the realization that no happiness could now come from it had long ago dawned on me.

Finally the austere grey buildings of the courts came into view. On legs that suddenly felt leaden I passed through the double doors into the intimidating interior. Barristers, solicitors and alleged criminals huddled in groups on seats that had been designed with neither aesthetics nor comfort in mind. I sat flanked on either side by the sergeant and his wife, wondering where my father was, but thankful I could not see him. I was waiting for the time I would be called to give evidence against him.

The mirror that morning had shown me a drawn, pale face, looking older than my fifteen years, framed by shoulder-length hair in a neat pageboy style. No make-up reduced my pallor or disguised the dark shadows beneath eyes that held no youthful optimism or the joyful expectancy of a teenager with her whole life before her. It was the face of a girl in whom all hope and trust had, if not died, been abandoned for that day.

Tea was brought to me as we waited, then the internal door of the court opened to release the black-suited clerk of the court, whom I knew by sight. He approached me hurriedly and informed me that my father had already given his evidence and pleaded guilty, so I would not have to be cross-examined. He told me that the judge had a few questions to put to me though, and then he ushered me in.

A Bible was produced for me to swear, 'to tell the whole truth and nothing but the truth'. I was shown where to stand and turned to face the bewigged judge who, with a kindly smile, asked me if I wanted to sit, which gratefully I did. My mouth was dry and the judge instructed water to be passed to me. I took small sips, letting it slide down my suddenly dry throat.

'Antoinette,' he commenced, 'I just want you to answer a few questions, then you will be free to go. Just answer them to the best of your ability. And remember that you are not on trial here. Can you do that?'

Overawed by his white wig and scarlet gown, I whispered, 'Yes.'

'Did you at any time tell your mother?'

I replied in the negative.

His next question took me by surprise and I felt an awareness in the room that had not been there before. 'Do you know the facts of life? Do you know how women become pregnant?' he asked.

Again I whispered, 'Yes.'

'Then surely you must have been scared of becoming pregnant?'

I looked into his face and knew, without understanding why, that the answer to this was important.

'He always used something,' I answered at last and heard the sigh of my father's solicitor.

'What did he use?' was his last question.

'It looked like a balloon,' was my answer. With my lack of interest in boys, I had no need to know the word condom.

At the time I didn't realize that my answer had just confirmed premeditation. Those few words had ensured my father received a prison sentence and was not sent to the mental hospital as his solicitor had been hoping. The judge excused me and I, avoiding my father's gaze, left the courtroom to return to my seat in the waiting room, where I would have to sit until the judge had passed sentence and I had been told of the outcome.

Watching the doors of the courtroom for what seemed like hours, but can't have been more than fifteen minutes, I saw them open and my father's solicitor coming through them. He came to my side.

'Your father received four years,' he said. 'With good behaviour he'll be out in two and a half.' There was no emotion in his voice at the fate of his client. 'Your father wants to see you. He's in the holding cells – it's up to you if you want to. You don't have to.'

Trained as I was to obey, I agreed to go. He took me to where my father sat. All fear left me as I looked at the man who had tormented me for so many years and I waited for him to speak.

'You be looking after your mother now, Antoinette, do you hear?'

'Yes, Daddy,' I replied for the last time for many months. Then I turned and walked away, to go in search of the police sergeant and his wife.

'The judge wants to see you for a few minutes,' the sergeant informed me as the clerk of the court walked up to us and motioned me to follow him.

Moments later, for the second time that day, I faced the judge. This time it was in his rooms and he had already removed his wig and gown. He motioned me to take a seat. Looking at me gravely he told me his reasons for wanting to speak to me in private.

'Antoinette, you will find, as I know you already have, that life is not fair. People will blame you, as they already have. But I want you to listen to me very carefully. I've seen the police reports. I've seen your medical reports. I know exactly what has happened to you, and I'm telling you that none of this was your fault. You have done nothing to be ashamed of.'

Those words I stored safely away, ready to take them out when the need came.

A case that is held *in camera* might limit the number of people allowed inside a courtroom, but it can never silence the ones outside. Ambulance drivers, nurses, the police themselves, not to mention social workers and two teachers were all on my mother's list of suspects when she became aware that the whole town was talking.

Not only were they talking, they had taken sides. Coleraine, my father's staunch Protestant home town, blamed the child.

I was well developed, my shyness made me seem aloof and I spoke in a middle-class English accent, an accent that was far from popular in Ulster then. My father, on the other hand, was a local man, one who had fought in the war, come home with medals and was seen as a hero by his family. With no conscription in Northern Ireland every man who had fought in the Second World War was a brave volunteer. They felt his mistake was in his choice of wife, a woman not only five years older than him, but one who looked down on his friends and family. He was the good sport in the pubs, a champion amateur golfer and a brilliant snooker player, a man liked and respected by men and women alike.

'Paedophile' was not a word bandied about then, nor was it the one they would have attached to my father anyway. I was a willing party, they said, and to save myself when I fell pregnant I'd screamed rape. I'd taken my own father to court, testified against him and washed a very large family's dirty linen in public. With the case held *in camera* only some of the facts had come out but even if all of them had been printed in the papers I doubt if the town would have believed them. People, I learnt early, believe mainly what they want to, including the person telling the lies.

I first became aware of the town's reaction when I called on one of my father's cousins, Nora, a woman with a five-year-old daughter whom I was fond of. I'd baby-sat for the child and enjoyed playing with her on numerous occasions. Nora's door swung open and she stood with her hands on her hips and a glare on her face, while her daughter hid behind her skirts, her face peeking round.

'You've got a nerve coming round here. Do you think we'd let our daughter play with the likes of you? We know what you've done – we know all about your father and you.' Anger, coupled with disgust, almost made her choke as she spat the final words at me. 'Get yourself off my doorstep and don't come back.'

I reeled back as though hit, and the last sight of the little girl I had played with were her bewildered blue eyes looking up at me before the door slammed in my face. Stunned, I went home to the coldness of my mother. She had given up her job, she said, and was never going to leave the house. She could not bear the disgrace – it was in the papers. And it was. My name was not mentioned and naively I still thought that in some way that would protect me, but everyone knew and now it was officially confirmed.

My mother then told me she was putting the house on the market and we would move, not to England as I hoped, but to Belfast. We would move as soon as it was sold. In the meantime I could do all the shopping; she was not going to face the town and the gossip – I could deal with that. I could carry on at school until we left, as it would get me out of the house. She was wrong about that: the next day I was expelled.

There was a hush as I entered the school hall: girls avoided my eyes; girls who I thought were my friends turned away, except one. Lorna, my friend from Portstewart, a girl whose home I'd visited many times, met my eyes and smiled. Thinking she was still a friend I approached her. She gave me an embarrassed look, for she had been appointed as the spokesperson for the group. Although she looked far from happy with the task, I could see her determination to blurt out her prepared speech.

'My mother says I'm to have nothing to do with you.' Then she paused. 'I'm sorry, but we've all been told the same.'

I stood in the school grounds, holding my satchel to me, too numb to feel emotion, and saw the Deputy Head approaching.

'Antoinette, we did not expect you today. We've written to your mother. Did she not get our letter?'

I told her the post always came after I left for school and her only response was to purse her lips, while her small dark eyes slid from my face to a point over my shoulder. I stood silent, in the vain hope that I could delay what I knew was to come. Finally she spoke again. 'You can't attend this school. Your mother will get her letter today.' She must have seen the stricken look on my face as she looked at me with distaste, but her only answer to my silent appeal was another question.

'What did you expect after all your carrying on? We know about you and your father. We've had phone calls from parents, the board was consulted last night and we had a meeting about you. It's a unanimous decision: you're expelled. Your desk and locker have been cleared. Now follow me to my office and you can collect your possessions.'

Disgrace weighing me down, I rebelled and turned to her. 'It was not my fault,' I protested. 'He made me.'

'What, every time? Don't make things even worse.'

Then, with her unpleasant duty done, she escorted me to the gates.

'Don't try and contact any of the girls – their parents don't want them to have anything to do with you,' were her parting words, and I walked away from the building where for eight years I had spent the majority of my schooling. It was here that I had tentatively tried to make those early friendships, the sort of friendships that we hope once formed will last for life. I bit the inside of my cheek to stop myself from crying as I thought of what I could do to delay going home.

My mother, I knew, would have had her letter by now. What would her reaction be? I wondered miserably, dreading returning to her and the cold barrier that she had erected between us. A wall that I had never accepted had been steadily built, brick by brick, over the eight years since I was six. Now it was impossible to scale. Since I'd told her of my pregnancy the final brick had been laid and the coldness showed that with it the last threads of any love she might once have felt had now died. I walked, clutching my satchel stuffed full now with the extra books from my desk. Surely, I thought miserably, my grandmother would welcome me as she loved me, and with that hope my steps took me to her house.

She let me in, and then went to the kitchen to make tea. No question was asked of why I was there on a school morning and that warned me what the next few minutes would bring. She gave me a cup of tea at the table and she sat down opposite me. She looked careworn, dragged down by her son's guilt and the decision she felt had to be made. She broke the family's conclusion as to the best way to handle the situation as gently as she could.

'I knew you would come here today. I know what Nora is planning to say to you.' She must have seen by the expression on my face that I had already paid a visit to my father's cousin's house. She sighed and her hand came over the table to cover mine.

'Antoinette, listen to me. Your father is my eldest son, and what he did was wrong – I know that, but we cannot have you visit us again.'

I stared at her bleakly. She was speaking the words that deep down I had been dreading hearing. I put my cup down and asked her a question I already knew the answer to. 'Do all of you feel the same?'

'Yes, go back to your mother. It would be better if she took you to England. It's where you both belong.'

And that was her goodbye to me, because I never saw her again.

I squared my shoulders and for the first time did not kiss

her goodbye. Instead I walked out of her house and up the street, where not one person greeted me. I thought of the warmth of my grandparents' home, the love I'd received there. I remembered her smiles of welcome when we had returned from England and saw the sag of her shoulders as the realization of what her son had done sunk in. I already felt the loss of my family for I knew they were gone for ever. I realized that over the years he would be forgiven but I, once loved but not as much as him, would not. Having nowhere left to go, I forced that final loss to the back of my mind and went home to confront my mother.

The weeks before the house and my father's car were sold passed in coldness, until even running the gauntlet of the stares and muttering of the town as I did our shopping was preferable to staying at home. I had expected at least some understanding, even sympathy, from the adult world but in the end small kindnesses came only from the most unexpected places. Our next-door neighbours, who must have heard some of the sounds of my father's temper filtering into their house in the past, invited us for supper. The husband offered to help with any odd jobs that might be needed round the house so we would get the best price for it and his wife offered to help with packing. The next person was the owner of our local shop, the only person who spoke directly to me.

'You're always welcome in here,' he told me. 'I've heard the stories and I want to tell you my viewpoint is different from most you've come across. If anyone is rude to you in here they can leave my shop. They know that too.'

Nobody was – they just treated me as though I was invisible as I, with my chin up, not looking to right or left, selected our purchases.

My mother kept her word and, apart from the occasional visit to our neighbours, whom up to then she had always felt herself superior to, she never left the house to venture out in Coleraine. Not until it was sold and we were free to move to Belfast did she tell me what her plans were. She had organized the rental of a small house in the notorious Shankhill district, for that was all we could afford now. She could not return to England: she had no intention of her family finding out where her husband was, and for the same reason I could not leave. I would have to find work in Belfast, a reality which I had already come to terms with. I would, I had decided, look for a job living-in, which would have two benefits. It would give me independence and get me away from my mother. Judy, I realized, would not be able to come with me and I knew how much I would miss her, but my mother loved her too and I knew she would look after the little dog if I was not there to do it. My need to escape the constant guilt I felt outweighed every other emotion. My long-cherished dream of living with my mother without my father had become a nightmare. I still loved her, longed for her to show me some understanding and affection, but she, caught up in her own depression, had none to give me. Two months after the court case we made our move and arrived in Belfast.

I thought the streets of tiny red-bricked houses, their doors opening straight onto the road, looked similar to my grandparents' area, but bigger and more interesting. Here there were numerous shops, a pub on every corner and a constant flow of people. Predictably, my mother hated it at first sight. This, she felt, was the end of her dream of life in Ireland; this was rock bottom and she was there through no fault of her own. Now a slow rage, fuelled by her resentment of life, seemed to burn in her. A resentment not just of the position she was in but also towards me. I let two days pass then told her that now we were unpacked I was starting my job-hunting the next day.

Chapter Twenty-Seven

In the morning I eagerly scanned the newspaper's situations vacant column, ringing around all the advertisements that stated accommodation would be provided. I wanted to get out of the house as soon as possible. Then, armed with a bag of coins, I walked to the nearby phone box.

The first number I rang was answered by a friendly lady who informed me that she wanted help with her two small children. As she and her husband had a busy social life, there would be on average four nights of baby-sitting duties, which was why accommodation was provided. She asked me if that would be a problem. I assured her I had no wish to go out at nights, except to visit my mother. We arranged an interview for later that day.

Feeling a sense of accomplishment that not only had I arranged an interview, but I might also soon have my own accommodation, I went home to choose a suitable outfit. I settled on a navy skirt with matching twin-set which, after checking for creases, I laid out on my bed. I polished my black kitten-heeled shoes until I could see my face in them, then selected clean undies and checked my stockings for runs.

Once I was satisfied my outfit was ready, I went down to the kitchen, where I boiled saucepans of water to shampoo my neatly cut hair and to have a strip wash. Looking into the age-spotted mirror propped against the wall by the kitchen sink, I carefully applied my make-up. A dab of matt foundation carefully blended in, a sweep of mascara, followed by a pale pink lipstick.

Knowing that my old school was unlikely to give me references, once I'd dressed I placed my last school report, which both praised my scholastic abilities and my exemplary behaviour, into my bag. I hoped these would satisfy my potential employer and she would not find the need to ask for further written confirmation. I had carefully rehearsed my story of why an 'A stream' pupil was looking for work as an au pair, over and over again in my mind, until I thought it sounded believable.

Giving one last look in the mirror to satisfy myself with my appearance, I picked up my bag and, armed with my private school accent, my school reports and my well-rehearsed lies, I left the house.

The first bus I had to catch took me into the centre of Belfast, then a short walk to another stop, where I was taken to the more fashionable Malone Road area. Nearby, I knew, was the university that I'd now accepted I would never be able to attend.

When I reached my destination, I walked the short distance to the house I had directions for. Before I had time to knock the door was flung open by a pretty, smiling young woman in her early twenties. She was holding a chubby toddler in her arms, of indeterminate sex, only the blue romper suit giving me a clue. The second child, a small girl, sucking the thumb of one hand, clutched a fold of her mother's skirt with the other as she surveyed me with curiosity.

'Can't shake hands,' the young woman laughed as she stood aside for me to enter. 'You must be Toni. I'm Rosa. Come on in.'

I followed her into a pretty pastel-coloured room that was dominated by a large playpen. Bending down she gently placed the toddler inside it, motioned me to a chair and seated herself, carefully appraising me.

Rosa, friendly as she was, obviously had a list of questions for anyone she was going to be trusting some of the care of her children to. I hoped I could pass her test. The first question, where I had gone to school, I had expected and answered matter of factly. To the second one, why I had left so young, I had ready my rehearsed answer. I omitted the numerous schools I had attended and gave her the impression that I had only attended one. I explained I had not been a scholarship pupil, which prepared me for my biggest lie. My father had tragically died some months previously, leaving very little money. I further embellished on that fiction by telling her the only reason my mother and I had made the move from Coleraine to Belfast was to seek work.

Seeing sympathy growing in her eyes, I threw in my final lines with confidence.

My mother had not only lost her husband, but had now been forced by lack of money to move from her pleasant house to the less salubrious Shankhill Road. My wish, I explained, was to help with her rent, which I felt I could only do if I was living in, thus removing all responsibility of my upkeep from my mother's shoulders.

It worked far better than I had hoped for. I knew before I put the icing on the cake by producing my school reports that the job was mine, and my fear that written references would be asked for were groundless. After another hour of chatting and getting to know her two children, baby David and Rachael, it was arranged for me to move in with my belongings the next day. Rosa would then spend time with me, showing me my duties.

In the evening she and her husband, who she had proudly explained to me was a busy doctor, would often be dining out. When they were absent, my job would be to put the children to bed, and then I would be allowed to watch television in their sitting room.

As I returned home that afternoon, I felt a sense of freedom. I knew that Rosa and her children had liked me. For the first time in many months I thought I had met people who had judged me for the person I was, not for what they knew about me. What I did not understand was that whereas the children liked me for who I was, Rosa liked the person I had invented for her: Toni the well brought up teenager who had not, as I had told her, even had a boyfriend. She had liked a girl whose interests were reading and animals, whose sole ambition was to learn to be a children's nanny and whose one desire was to help her widowed mother. I had described my extended Irish family, where I had learnt my childcare skills, but omitted to mention that I was now banished from their homes.

The feeling of confidence lasted me over my two bus journeys and did not waver when I let myself into our small house. My mother was already home and I knew, with a sinking heart, that her air of despondency meant that her job interview must have been futile.

'Mummy,' I blurted out, 'I've got a job. It's living in and I start tomorrow. It pays three pounds a week plus my board, so I can help you with money.'

She looked uncomprehendingly at me. 'What will you be doing?' she enquired after a few minutes.

'Looking after children and helping with housework,' I replied, knowing what was going to come next.

'Oh, Toni, and I had such hopes for you,' she exclaimed, making me feel guilty for having let her down again.

It was that guilt that made me even more determined to leave. So, ignoring her last remark, I talked with an enthusiasm that I was beginning to lose about Rosa, the children and the nice house I would live in.

'I'll eat with the family when they're in,' I continued.

'Not if they knew about you, you wouldn't,' she flatly informed me. 'Still, no doubt you'll enjoy watching television. I would too, if I could afford one.'

On the surface I refused to let my mother's depression reach me, but underneath I still longed for some affection, some warmth; but none came. From being the dutiful teenager in Rosa's eyes, I was now the selfish daughter in my mother's.

We sat silently around the tiny sitting room, listening to the radio and reading. After a light supper, I went upstairs to pack my few belongings.

Rosa had pressed some coins on me for my travelling expenses, so at least I did not have to ask my mother for any money the next morning. Standing at the door, I looked at her as I struggled with the feelings that I had not yet learnt to suppress, but found impossible to show.

'I'll see you next week on my day off,' I said eventually, as I picked up my suitcase, opened the door and left. She, as usual, said nothing.

Arriving at my new home, Rosa showed me to my room, where I quickly unpacked before eagerly going down to the kitchen to find my charges. I had my first lesson in feeding the under-fours, which brought back memories of helping with my little cousin when she was the same age.

I soon found that my routine was an easy one. On my first evening, before I bathed the children, I was introduced to Rosa's husband, David senior, who gravely shook my hand and told me he hoped I would be happy with them.

Bathing the children resulted in squeals of delightful laughter as I turned floating toys into submarines and made them dive under the soap-sudded children. Hearing the noise, David and Rosa, dressed for the evening, came to say their goodnights. Avoiding the suds, they kissed their two children goodbye, then left me in charge.

That first evening, as in the following ones, I scooped the plump, wriggling little bodies out of the bath, wrapped them in fluffy towels and rubbed them vigorously dry. I wondered if, with a promise of one last read, they would go uncomplaining to their bedroom. First baby David was placed in his cot, and then I would tuck the little girl into bed, reading them a story of Rachael's choosing. When their eyes began to droop, I dropped kisses onto their heads before going downstairs to watch television.

Over the next few weeks I developed a deep affection for the children. When I played with him, baby David would grasp one of my fingers in his plump hand, giving me a toothless grin, which would almost split his face in two. Rachael would sit on my lap with a grave look of concentration on her face as I read to her. When I took David's pram to the park, she would help me push, but one hand always held mine.

Six days a week I would make them their lunch, which I ate with them. Often, when the children had their afternoon naps, Rosa and I would talk. Sometimes we would sit in her bedroom, where she would model newly bought clothes, seeking my opinion.

Lulled into the warmth of this family, I began to fantasize I was part of it. I let myself forget that Rosa, although friendly to me, was not a friend, and that she and her husband were my employers. I tried to win Rosa's affection by offering to do extra tasks such as making her tea or helping with the ironing. She, on the other hand, seemed vaguely amused by my attentions; certainly she did nothing to discourage them.

The house always felt happy. It was clear that David and Rosa were not only loving parents, but cared deeply for each other as well. They reminded me of my Aunt Catherine's family and as each day passed I felt lucky to be there. I knew always to be upstairs or in the kitchen with the children when David came home as I sensed he and his wife valued time together on his return. I had observed how, when she heard the sound of his car as it drove up the short driveway, she would rush to open the door for him.

Knowing this, I was surprised one evening, when they had no plans to go out, that they both came into the bathroom. I was kneeling, bathing the children. I sensed their presence before I heard David's voice.

'Antoinette,' I dimly heard. 'That is your name, isn't it?'

I looked up at him and he saw the truth in my eyes.

'My wife will take over from you. I will speak to you downstairs.'

Everything felt in slow motion. I stood up on legs that trembled as I tried to catch Rosa's eye to seek some help there, but she averted her flushed face from my gaze. Feeling the adults' tension, my two young charges looked up in bewilderment, their faces turned up to me, wondering why I had suddenly stopped playing with them.

I slowly put down the soapy sponge that was dripping

onto the floor, and then mutely followed him downstairs to the sitting room. Not motioned to sit, I stood facing him, seeing on his face the stony look I had seen so often before on other people's faces.

'Your father is not dead, is he?' he pointlessly asked me in a tone of voice that told me he knew the answer. 'He's in prison and you're lucky not to be in a home. Well, you're certainly not staying in this home for one more night. Go straight to your room and pack, then stay there until I come for you. I'll drive you to your mother's.'

I tried to defend myself. 'It was not my fault, the judge said so.' I blurted out, desperate for him to believe me and allow me to stay.

A look of such revulsion and contempt crossed his face so that I felt myself wither inside.

'Well, it is not his children you're looking after, is it? You kept quiet for seven years; it was only your need for an abortion that made you talk. You even lied to your doctor who I have spoken to this afternoon. Your school expelled you because other parents quite rightly judged you unfit to mix with their children.' I could sense the anger mounting in him. 'I want you out of here tonight!' He spoke with such finality that I knew my happy life there was finished.

As I walked out of the room, I heard his voice again, following me. 'Rosa agrees with me, in case you think differently. She does not want to see you, so go straight to your room.'

I went, willing myself not to cry. That would come later, in private, I told myself.

Rosa's bedroom door was shut, but behind it I could hear the murmur of her voice, interspersed with the higher-pitched tones of Rachael. I knew she had taken the children in there to avoid me.

The next half an hour passed in a daze as I packed my few belongings, then sat on the edge of my bed as I waited for David's knock.

'You have everything?' were the only words he spoke to me after he fetched me from my room, put me firmly in the back seat of the car, along with my suitcase, and drove away from the leafy suburban area of the Malone Road to the narrow, dimly lit streets of the Shankhill Road area. When we reached my mother's house, holding my arm firmly, he knocked on the door and waited for her to open it before releasing me. In the light of the single hanging bulb in the doorway, a resigned look came over my mother's face.

'I'm returning your daughter, Mrs Maguire,' was all he said before he turned back to his car and drove away.

The witching hour came, bringing a wave of misery that engulfed me. I heard my father's voice in my ears: 'Your mother won't love you if you talk. Everyone will blame you.' I now knew with absolute certainty that what he predicted was true. I conjured up one kind face, that of the judge, hearing his voice as he told me, 'You are not to blame, remember that, because people will blame you.'

Wearily, I climbed out of bed, splashed cold water onto my face and dressed hurriedly. For the second time in a few months I walked to the newsagents to purchase the local paper. Taking it to a nearby coffee shop I ringed around the situations vacant that required no qualifications and offered accommodation, frightened of phoning someone who might know David and Rosa.

One advertisement stood out: 'Large country house needs au pair to help with two pre-school children. Accommodation to be provided, good wages for right applicant.'

After I rang to make my appointment for the late afternoon of that day, I dressed in the same clothes I'd worn all those weeks ago to my first interview. This time I felt no excitement, no feeling of starting a new life, just a dull acceptance of what I now knew the future held for me. Again I took the bus into central Belfast, and then changed to the one that would take me to my country destination. On my arrival I saw not the overgrown hedges and tall trees from my memories of Cooldaragh, but neatly boxed hedges lining a drive which led to a square grey Georgian house, its high narrow windows facing the manicured green lawns. No overgrown rhododendron bushes for children to play in here, no trickling stream where frogs could be found. Instead, circles of earth planted with rose bushes provided the only splashes of colour to break up the uniform green.

Nor was there a smiling Rosa with her twinkling eyes answering the bell to me. Instead a cool-looking blonde, as manicured as her lawns, opened the door. As she led me through the hall into her colour-coordinated sitting room, with roses arranged in crystal vases standing on small mahogany tables, I wondered where the children were.

My unspoken question was answered when she told me they were in the nursery with her temporary help.

Once again my rehearsed story worked its magic; once again it was agreed that I would move into a room arranged as a bed-sitter, and my wages would be £3 per week. This time I would have a television in my room, not being part of a family here, but it was agreed I would eat my evening meal with them. After these formalities had been gone through, I was taken to meet my two charges, a boy and a girl again, both with the blonde good looks of their mother. I thought then that in such an organized household boy first, girl second was just what they would have ordered.

While waiting for her husband, plates of crust-less sandwiches were brought into the sitting room by a maid. Tea from a large silver pot was poured into thin china cups, sugar being added with small silver tongs, as I perched on the edge of a velvet wing-back chair. She told me that her husband was a merchant banker, that her last au pair had gone to England and that she wanted someone to stay until both children reached school age in one year and two respectively.

I agreed to that – after all what choice did I have? But already I knew that she and I would never be friends. I was just a paid servant to her. Then I wondered if maybe that was better. At least I would not be under any illusion that I was part of a family that was not mine.

Briefly, before my departure, I was introduced to her husband, a tall slim man in his early thirties, whose polite smile did not reach his eyes.

Again, I caught the two buses to my mother's, repacked my suitcase and told her about my new job. For once she seemed happy: she had finally found work, she informed me, as manageress of a coffee shop. She told me how much she liked the owner, an enthusiastic young man of twenty-eight, who had just started his own business.

In the smart Georgian house, the cold loneliness of my isolation seemed to penetrate my skin. As each day passed I felt increasingly benumbed. I would eat with the family most evenings, and then go to my room to either read or watch television. This family I felt no bond with. I still missed Rosa and her children, and the warmth I'd felt in their home.

On my fourth day off, knowing that my mother was working, I went to visit her at the coffee shop. She was transformed: a new short hairstyle, carefully applied make-up, matching red lipstick and nail varnish all gave her a youthful, modern appearance. She smiled brightly at me, but the love I was searching for was not in her eyes.

'What are you doing here?' she asked.

'Can we have coffee together?' I said, but I was thinking, 'I'm here because I miss you.'

'Oh, darling,' she replied, 'of course we can have a quick cup, but it's lunchtime soon, and we get really busy.'

We sat on the banquet seating, served by a young waitress in her deep pink and cream uniform, which was unlike most of the waitresses in Belfast then, who still wore black and white. My mother asked me how I liked my work and the family. I described everything to her in detail, the house, gardens and the children, but omitted to say that, while it was much grander than Rosa's and David's, it lacked the warmth and fun.

To my mother, I knew, I had described the house of her dreams, but to me it was a building rather than a home. Less than an hour later, after a quick hug and another bright smile from my mother, I was back on the pavement again with the rest of my free day stretching in front of me.

A kaleidoscope of faces with varying expressions from disdain to anger floated before me and their voices rang in my ears. First was my father's. His mocking smile as he told me time and again: 'Your mother won't love you if you tell. Everyone will blame you.' Next, my mother's black angry stare on the night I was bleeding to death, her whisper to the doctor as she told him to send me to the further hospital. My grandmother's stern expression, from which all traces of love had disappeared. The dislike that showed in my cousin Nora's face when she had opened the door, shielding her child from me. Their combined voices echoed in my head.

'Antoinette, you are not welcome. We know about you and your father. Go away, don't ever come back. Don't ever come back.'

I felt the pain of each rejection again. Tears misted my eyes as I relived that final one when David sent me packing from his home. The despair I had fought against when I had stood with my meagre possessions, hurriedly packed into my one small suitcase, returned and lodged inside me. Pride, my only remaining weapon, left me, and in its place grief and self-pity moved in. No longer could I see that elusive silver lining to the black cloud of my life. It was simply not there.

Nobody, I thought, could ever love me. No one ever had, not the real me. Oh yes, they had loved the pretty girl dressed in smock dresses, the clever child with good school reports, the helpful teenager, always ready to baby-sit. But who had loved the pregnant me, the sexually aware me, the frightened me? Not even my mother.

All around I could see groups of friends, or couples happy with each other. People, who belonged to families, people who were loved. I sat there, an isolated, invisible alien in an unwelcoming world, a world that I had only been happy in for the first six of my fifteen years. Momentary happiness had fleetingly come, but never stayed. Rejection, the hardest emotion to deal with, had put me in a mental cage. I had no door back into the world of people. The only door I could see was the one marked 'exit'.

Could I stay for ever in that cage where no love, companionship or even acceptance visited? The only answer to that was 'no', the only option to leave.

Knowing that whiskey dulled pain, I walked to the nearest pub. The invisible me ordered a double in that male-dominated refuge, and greedily drank it down. The barman saw a potential drunk and refused me a second one.

'What's the matter, love? Boyfriend trouble? You'll find another one, pretty girl like you.'

His words sounded like they came from somewhere far away. Paranoia joined despair and, instead of hearing kindness in his voice, I heard mocking tones of derision.

Leaving the warmth of the pub, gripped with a cold determination, I walked to the nearby chemist. There I bought a large bottle of aspirin and a packet of razor blades. The invisible me then walked to an off-licence and bought my last purchase, a bottle of Bush Mill's Whiskey. Armed with my exit kit, I went to a public toilet.

A pale face loomed in the mirror as I stood, toasting myself with the bottle, gulping down the whiskey and aspirins. The mixture rose back up my throat, my eyes streaming each time I choked. More whiskey and more tablets went down, until both bottles were emptied. I dropped them into the bin and entered a cubicle. I put down the seat and sat on it, then slowly opened the packet of razor blades. Selecting one, I cut into myself systematically, starting at the wrist and rising two inches above it. Fifteen slashes, one for each year of the life I no longer wanted. Blood slowly oozed down over my hands between my fingers, then dripped onto the floor. Mesmcrized, I watched its journey, wondering how long it would take my body to empty out. My lids became heavy and started closing as the world darkened and a buzzing set up in my ears. I felt myself slipping sideways, felt the cool of the wall where my head rested against it. Then I felt no more.

Chapter Twenty-Eight

Indistinct words from two voices penetrated my consciouness. The first a deep masculine one; the second the higher-pitched tones of a female.

'We know you're awake. Come on, open your eyes,' said the masculine voice.

A cool soft hand took mine, and I heard the female voice. 'Come on dear, we want to help you. Open your eyes now.'

Reluctantly I did as they asked.

I was lying in a bed in a small white room. My lips struggled to form words and I felt a peculiar sensation in my mouth; an object was stopping any sound escaping. My tongue touched something solid and hard. Then I realized this hard thing was sliding up from deep inside me, up into my throat and out through my lips.

Two people came into focus and I recognized that one was a nurse while the other, dressed in tweed jacket with a clerical collar, was a minister. Dimly I realized I was in a hospital, then gagged as a rush of vomit, hot and burning, rose in my throat. Hands placed a bowl under my head and now that the tube-like object, which later I learnt was a stomach pump, had done its job, my body heaved with the exertion of emptying all the toxins out.

When at last the attack was over, I lay back, hearing a constant ringing in my ears. A desire to sleep again made me close my eyes but the voices were not going to let me slip away so easily.

I heard them asking who I was and where I lived, but I hardly knew the answers to that myself. My hand was held, and liking the feeling of comfort it gave me, I gripped tightly.

'Come on, open your eyes again,' the minister said. 'We'll let you sleep when you've answered a few questions.'

I forced my lids apart again to find his kind blue eyes looking at me, with nothing but concern on his face. It was the kindness I saw there that made me cry, choking sobs that shook my body as much as the vomiting had. Still the nurse's hand held mine while his wiped my face.

I could hear comforting noises of the sort mothers usually make to their babies. Gradually I felt soothed, the crying stopped and when he asked me my name again I told him it was Antoinette, even though I had come to hate it. Antoinette was the name 'he' called me, the name his mother addressed me by and the name the school had used when they expelled me. Toni, the person I wanted to be, had managed to elude me.

The next question came: how old was I?

'Fifteen,' I told him and braced myself for the question I knew would follow.

'Antoinette, why did you do it?'

My eyes dropped to my hands and I saw the bandaged wrists. The compassion in his voice made me cry again, silently this time. Unchecked, the tears ran down my face until I managed to stutter out some of my story. I told them my father had gone to prison because he had made me pregnant, that I had no home and nobody wanted me. I did not want to live because I had nothing to live for.

I couldn't bring myself to open every wound, to tell them of all the rejection I had experienced, how it had made me feel so worthless, so unloved. Or the guilt I felt, because my mother's life was in ruins and I knew she blamed me for it. Neither did I talk about the dream I had nurtured, of my father being discovered and adults rushing to surround me with love and care. Nor did I tell them how I had dreamt of my mother whisking me away from him and taking me somewhere safe. The reality of what had followed the discovery of 'our secret' had been more than I could bear. I did not explain how the back of my neck tingled, or describe the sinking, sick sensations that crept into my stomach every time I went into a shop and felt the silence thicken. I always knew that the buzz of conversation I heard go up the moment I left was about me.

Gradually I had come to see myself through the eyes of others, someone to be ignored to such an extent that they would eventually disappear. I was someone so tainted that others feared that by even recognizing my existence they too would be sullied.

Not only did I have nothing, but I *was* nothing. And yet some tiny spark of pride still remained, stopping me from talking about those feelings. I never did; it was almost as if I hoped that by not verbalizing them I could make them cease to exist.

I heard the nurse's intake of breath and then she asked the next question.

'What happened to the baby?' Maybe she envisioned my having given birth and it being left in a doorway somewhere. It made me feel angry that she would think such a thing of me.

'They gave me an abortion,' I said baldly; fifteen-year-olds were not expected to use such words.

'Antoinette, if you were released would you try again?' the nurse asked, but neither of them bothered to wait for my answer – they knew what it would be.

The minister took the address of where I had worked and promised to collect my clothes, while the nurse gave me a cold drink and I fell into another sleep, still with the constant noises in my ears – the results of the poisons I had put into my body.

The next time I awoke another man was sitting by my bed.

'Antoinette, would you like a drink?' he asked gently as he saw my eyes flutter.

'Tea,' I croaked in reply. My tongue felt too big for my mouth and my throat hurt.

The buzzing was fainter but my head ached with a throbbing pain.

'Can I have a pain killer?' I asked weakly.

'That will have to get better naturally,' he replied. Then, as if deciding I deserved to be given a reason, he continued, 'We've spent some time pumping aspirin out of you.' He paused for a few moments before going on. 'Antoinette, I'm a doctor, but a doctor of the mind, a psychiatrist. Do you know what that means?'

I nodded. It was of no interest to me who he was: I just wanted to drink my tea and go back to sleep. He, however, had not finished what he wanted to say.

'I've arranged a transfer for you, to the local psychiatric hospital. They'll know how to treat you there. You're suffering from an illness; it's called severe depression.'

That was a statement I could agree with. He patted me on the shoulder, assured me I would feel better soon, and left. It was a reassurance I had no faith in. A few minutes later, still wrapped in hospital clothes, clutching my suitcase, which the minister had fetched for me, I was placed in an ambulance and made the short journey to Purdysburn mental hospital.

We drove past the massive red-brick structure, which in Victorian days had been a poorhouse but now housed the long-stay patients, to a single-storey building. This was their newest unit, the psychiatric section, where I was to be admitted. I was the youngest patient there by several years.

That first night I hardly took in my surroundings. Still

drowsy from the overdose, I slept until I was woken the following morning. The curtains around my bed were drawn and a cheerful voice told me to get up, wash and come to breakfast. I looked to see where the voice had come from and saw a young nurse with a smile so open and friendly that I found myself smiling back. Standing next to her was a tall, slim blonde-haired girl a few years older than me who the nurse introduced.

'This is Gus. She'll show you the ropes.'

With that she disappeared, leaving us alone. Gus's constant chatter, which I welcomed, washed over me. I could take refuge in silence because she only ever paused in order to take a breath or to emit a nervous, high-pitched laugh. This, I was soon to learn, was the flip side of depression.

She showed me the bathrooms, waited for me to wash and dress, then led me to the small dining room. As my disorientation gradually left me I became aware of my surroundings. Both the ward and the dining room were painted in pale colours, large windows letting light stream in, creating an airy, tranquil space. All the other patients were already seated and Gus quickly introduced me to the twenty or so people there. I'd heard horror stories of the mental hospitals; stories about how, once admitted, people could disappear into the system and never emerge. But I'd never been told about the psychiatric unit, a fairly new venture.

Everyone looked so normal. The patients of both sexes ranged from late teens to early fifties and, I was soon to learn, came from all walks of life. Depression and alcohol abuse, the two main reasons why they had been admitted, had no respect for either age or class.

Over the weeks I spent there I learnt most of their stories. There was the wealthy estate agent's wife, who had been made to feel inferior by her husband's philandering and secretly drank. Like me she had taken an overdose. Unlike me, however, hers was an accident. Her mind dulled by gin, she forgot how many tranquillizers she'd taken and kept repeating the dose. Then there was a young couple who had met in the unit a year before. They were both being treated for alcohol abuse when they met, fell in love and discharged themselves. But instead of walking off hand-in-hand into the sunset they walked to the nearest pub.

Some patients were sitting quietly, their tranquillizers keeping their brains sluggish while the doctors waited for their depression to lift and control to pass from the drugs to the person. One woman especially caught my attention. With a mass of bright red hair, creamy skin and green eyes she was the prettiest member of the group and the quietest.

I felt my eyes being drawn to her constantly throughout the meal. She, however, never met my gaze, eating her meal with downcast eyes. She seemed completely unaware of both her surroundings and her fellow patients and her blank indifference aroused my interest.

At the end of the meal a nurse came to her table, gently took her by the arm and led her back to the ward. There she was placed in a chair, her knees covered by a blanket as she gazed mutely into space while the hours passed.

My curiosity was piqued and at the first opportunity I asked Gus who she was.

'She's the wife of a doctor,' she told me. 'If she wasn't she wouldn't be in this ward any more.'

'What's wrong with her?' I asked.

'Don't know, but some women get very depressed when they have a baby and she's been in here for over a year. When she came here she spoke, but she doesn't even do that any more.'

'Will she get better?' but even as the question left my lips I knew she wouldn't.

For some reason this mattered to me. This woman, whom I had never met before, had aroused my curiosity and my pity. I knew about that space we can go to where the world no longer touches us and reality drifts away, but instinctively I knew her space was in a far deeper place than mine had ever been.

'Well, if she doesn't, she'll get transferred; that's what happens if we don't respond to treatment.' Gus seemed indifferent to the woman's fate and, not wanting to know where she would be taken to, I ceased my enquiries.

After breakfast I was questioned about my medical history by the staff nurse and told not to leave the ward as the doctor would want to see me to assess my treatment and prescribe, if needed, any drugs. An hour later I had the first of many meetings with a psychiatrist. He took copious notes as I talked but then, just when I was beginning to relax with him, asked the one question that made any future rapport between us impossible.

'Antoinette, did you ever enjoy your father's advances?'

Even when I replied, 'Never,' he still persisted.

'Surely,' he said, 'you are a teenager, so you must have had some desires.'

At that moment I switched off, letting his voice float in the air, making my mind go blank so that his words could not affect me. I did not tell him about the town that had made me an outcast, how I felt worthless and demeaned, how I still wanted my mother's love, or how I thought my life had no hope. Nor did I confide that inside I had screamed with pain at the rejections and numerous slights I'd received. How I had temporarily forgotten the judge's words and seen myself through my accusers' eyes as contemptible. Instead I found another mask – no longer the one of the well-behaved schoolgirl and happy family member, but of someone suspicious of authority and indifferent to help.

They gave me tests to measure my IQ, and asked me if I heard voices in my head, voices that commanded me to take various actions. The last question was: did I feel people were talking about me?

'I don't think it,' I retorted, 'I know it.'

But that just evoked a supercilious smile and a flutter of his hand as he wrote busily. I found out later that the report said I was surly, uncooperative and paranoid.

Because of my age they decided to treat me without drugs and, even more importantly, without electric shocks. Instead therapy was prescribed on a daily basis.

At every hour-long session one of the three psychiatrists

assigned to my case asked me questions about my feelings and thoughts, which I answered as briefly as I could. My depression I hid under a protective screen of indifference. The one question to which I would never give them the answer they wanted was, 'Had I enjoyed any of the sex?'

They kept on asking the same thing. I think they thought I had and that only by confessing would I start to get better. They were not trying to be unkind, I knew that; they just had their preconceived ideas and refused to accept the truth. Did they really imagine I thought that being beaten, having whiskey poured down my throat and suffering mental torture was enjoyable?

How long had I been depressed was another often repeated question. How long did they think, I wanted to shout at them. When my life changed at six would have been the correct answer; but I knew it was not the one they wanted to hear. A few weeks was what I told them. I'd learnt exactly what could happen to a patient they thought was a danger to themselves or incurable: transfer to a locked ward and a disappearance from life as we know it.

Outside our insular unit lay the red-brick building of the old poorhouse with its small, mean, barred windows and its long dark corridors smelling of disinfectant and must. Surrounding this mass of bricks were single-storey buildings where, depending on the severity of the mental illness, long-term patients dressed in hospital uniforms lived. We often saw them being herded into groups as they were taken for their daily exercise by baton armed nurses.

A mental hospital in those days was a community isolated from the outside world, where it was felt that all the inmates' needs were catered for. It had a shop and a canteen, which we were allowed to visit. But each time I went, I returned disheartened. This seemed like a village of lost souls: people who nobody wanted and who had long been forgotten.

The massive hospital stood some distance from the main road, dwarfing all the more recently constructed buildings dotted around the extensive grounds. Sometimes, when the doors opened to release a convoy of blank-eyed inmates, either starting their walks or going to their dining rooms, I would get a peek inside one of the wards. There were cot-like beds and wooden chairs. Seated on some of them were the patients too unfit to even walk in the grounds. They rocked backwards and forwards on their chairs, moaning softly.

It was after I had my first glimpse of what life was like for the patients not considered well enough for the psychiatric unit that I realized how lucky we were to be placed there. Not only was the decoration fresh and modern but we had television, a games room and the kitchen was unlocked twenty-four hours a day, so we could make hot drinks whenever we felt like it and take them to one of the comfortable chairs nearby. We could sit and gaze out of the unbarred windows, browse through books or go for walks whenever we felt like it. The only restrictions were that we walked in groups for safety and were in the unit when our therapy was due. We were forbidden to leave the grounds unless we had permission, which would only be granted if we were accompanied by a visitor. We were never tempted to disobey that rule and visit the outside world because we had no wish to leave the safety and companionship of the hospital.

Visiting hours in our ward were also relaxed. As long as the visitors departed before the last night-time drinks were served there was no strict time of arrival and departure. I looked for my mother each day for the first six days I spent there. Had I been forgotten by the only person I had left, I would ask myself in despair as each evening failed to bring her. Once I realized it was too late for her to arrive that day I would retreat to my bed from where, with the curtains partly drawn around me, I would observe my fellow patients as they sat with their visitors grouped around their beds. I would affect a look of indifference and hold a book for comfort.

Each night I saw the red-haired woman's husband and their two little boys, one still in nappies. The children had her hair and eyes. On every visit he would hold her hand and talk while the children sat with their colouring books and toys and I would feel both his despair and the bewilderment that hung over all three of them. She would sit, unmoving, a small expressionless smile on her face. Not once did she speak. She no longer had any choice about staying in that space where reality had no meaning, but I began to realize that I still did. Watching them, I felt a small spark of optimism kindle inside me, and although I knew how easy it would be to let go, disappear into myself until I was like the red-haired woman, I no longer wanted to do that. Somewhere that strength that belongs to youth was returning.

My mother arrived on the Sunday carrying fruit, paperback books, magazines and flowers. I felt such a surge of love for her that it hurt. Later I found out that the hospital had phoned her and asked her why she hadn't visited. I was still a minor and would have to live with her on my release. Charmingly she had confirmed her concern; the only thing that had stopped her visiting, she had told them, was that she was working. As a manageress she had to supervise the staff in the evenings, but of course she was planning to visit on Sunday, her only free day. With only one wage coming in she could not afford to take extra time off and she knew I would understand.

The staff nurse, who tried to look as understanding as my mother expected me to be, informed me of the situation and I, blindly loyal to my mother, agreed it would be difficult.

Seeing her coming into the unit, I rushed to meet her and received a hug in return, the first one in a long time. She told me how worried she'd been about me, and how I was in the best place for the time being. Then she told me how much she liked her job. She had made plans for us both, she continued. I was not to live in other family's homes. It was the way they had treated me, she was sure, that had caused my breakdown. Then she said what I most wanted to hear: I could work in the coffee shop as a waitress when I was better, and live with her till I was older. She had seen a house, she continued – a pretty little gate lodge which, with my wages as well as hers, we could afford. Waitresses where she worked made more than she did as the manageress, because the coffee shop catered for businessmen, who were generous with their tips, especially to pretty, nicely brought-up girls like me, she added, with one of her warm bright smiles that I had not seen for so long.

That was the first time since I was a small child that my mother had paid me a compliment and I glowed with pleasure. I chattered to her as I had not done for so long, and told her about some of the other patients I was friendly with. When visiting time came to an end I happily waved her off, wishing I did not have to wait a whole week for her return.

The weeks I spent in the hospital passed quickly, because although our days were not particularly structured, they always seemed to be full. It was in there that I made a friendship that was to last for several years; my friend's name was Clifford. He'd heard about my past and with my bandaged wrists he, like everyone else, knew what I had tried to do. It was a platonic relationship, which suited both of us. He had little, if any, sexual interest in women and repressed any other desires he felt; a fact that had caused the departure of his wife and his subsequent breakdown. This he had told me on some of our walks together, sensing that, unlike his wife, I would find that particular confession reassuring.

My depression began to lift, helped by the constant company, Clifford's friendship and my mother's now more frequent visits. I felt there was a direction in my life; I had a home to go to, a job waiting for me, a life to start.

Three months after I had been admitted to Purdysburn my mother collected me.

Chapter Twenty-Nine

Within a few days I had my interview with the owner of the coffee shop, a young man whom I could see felt lucky to have my mother as manager and who offered me work straight away.

I was given my uniform of a peach-coloured overall and a cream apron and, to my relief, found the work easy. As my mother had told me, the tips were good. I was able to go to the hairdresser's and buy new clothes, as well as give my mother money. She, seeing that more cash was coming into the house, went ahead with her plans to buy the gate lodge. The small mortgage on it was easily covered by my extra contribution.

Nearly two years of peace followed, my father's name was never mentioned, nor was my breakdown, and she and I once again were close. There were evenings when we were both free. Being ardent film lovers we would often visit a cinema together, then spend hours discussing the various merits of each film we saw. Without my father's presence we no longer had to sit through westerns but could choose exactly the ones we liked.

On other occasions I would meet her from her shift and we would go for a coffee at a nearby café. There we would sit and chat as two women do. For I was at an age when I felt part of the adult world; certainly I felt I was contributing towards it. I was convinced that without my father's company my mother had finally grown to enjoy mine, a feeling that made me more and more satisfied as the weeks went on. Without his dark presence and his jealousy of any attention I received, I could show the love that I had always felt for her. Like a flower that seeks sunlight to grow strong, I needed the freedom to show love in order to flourish. Being able to do so in numerous ways filled me with such happiness that I was perfectly content to spend most of my free time with her.

During that time I felt very little need for other company. Sometimes I would cook our evening meal, lay the table and take pleasure simply from watching her eat a meal prepared from my latest recipe book. Although we both enjoyed reading and listening to music we also spent many evenings happily watching our newly acquired television, which was still a novelty to us. It only had two available channels so we seldom disagreed on which one to watch. There we would sit in front of a crackling fire, she in her favourite wing armchair, me curled up on the settee with Judy at my side. When our programme ended I would leap up to make us both a hot drink before going to bed.

Other times I would scour the small antique shops that had sprung up in Smithfield Market, to find her an unusual ornament, or a piece of jewellery.

Friends I'd made, such as Clifford, accepted that not only was my mother an important part of my life but that I also wanted her included in any social activities. I would present new friends to her in the hope she would like them and be entertained by them, because I felt her loneliness and wanted to protect her.

The only area of discontent lurking inside me was the knowledge that I didn't always want to be a waitress. I wanted to achieve something better, not just for myself but also for my mother. I wanted to make her proud of me, wanted to get a good job, one that would enable me to take care of her.

Just before my sixteenth birthday I resolved to do something about it. I had relinquished my ambition to go to university, knowing that three years out of the workplace would put too much of a strain on our joint finances. Without the much-needed money that I brought into the house my mother would not be able to make the mortgage payments.

Another option would be to take a secretarial course that would give me a school-leaving certificate stating a leaving age of eighteen, an age that prospective employers would find more acceptable than my present one of fourteen. I had already enquired about the cost of putting myself through a private college and worked out that, if I could get time off from the coffee shop during the summer to work in holiday locations for the season, I could save enough money for the fees in a few months. I did not foresee any problems with that arrangement since Belfast, being a university town, had no shortage of students ready to fill my role in their holidays while I worked away. I knew I would have to have enough savings to carry me through two terms, then I could repeat the plan the following year.

Once decided on my course of action I went to talk to the owner of the coffee shop.

There would be no problem, he assured me, and in fact he could help me out sooner. He had a distant cousin who owned a boarding house, grandly called 'a hotel', in the Isle of Man. She would be looking for staff over Easter and with his recommendation I could easily be placed there. The work would be harder than I was used to, he warned me: in a small establishment such as hers not only did the two waitresses she employed have to serve breakfast and evening meals but also clean the bedrooms and serve early morning teas.

Wages were not high but the tips were very good and I should be able to make more than twice the amount I made with him. If it worked out, I would be employed again in the summer.

Two weeks later, with promises to phone regularly, I caught the ferry to the Isle of Man.

Work in the hotel was hard with only two waitresses working as general dogsbodies. We would rise at seven-thirty, make the morning teas, and then climb the three flights of stairs to deliver them. Next, breakfast was served and only when the last dish was cleared could we sit down for ours. Lunch was not catered for in the weekly rate and we assumed that would be our free time. The owner, a short, overweight woman with dyed blonde hair sprayed stiffly into a backcombed helmet, had other ideas.

The silver had to be cleaned once a week, she informed us. Her voice, wheezing from her incessant smoking, would follow us wherever we went as, on short stubby legs, she would puff and snap at our ankles, seemingly frightened that without her supervision items would disappear or work would be left undone.

When holidaymakers had to be booked in, she would greet them with a charming smile, which would be replaced by a glare of impatience at us the moment the guests were looking the other way. We were never able to move fast enough to grasp their suitcase handles before she barked out her instructions to show the newly arrived families to their room. We would struggle up the steep staircase with luggage that seemed to weigh as much as us, then no sooner had we descended than tea had to be made.

New arrivals needed refreshments to revive them after their journeys more than we needed a rest, she informed us testily when we once had the temerity to ask for a break. We were young, she continued, while she had a bad heart. Did we not want to earn our tips, she asked us and, cowed, we refrained from introducing the subject again.

Her bad heart, I noticed, did not force her to abstain from smoking, or from eating large portions of puddings. Every time I heard her opining how she could not carry anything heavy, I thought sourly 'except yourself'.

Every day I looked at her flushed face with increasing dislike and wondered how anyone as charming as the coffee-shop owner could have such a dragon as a relative.

Some of the husbands would protest at a girl being asked to carry their suitcases, only to meet her frosty gaze as she icily informed them that we were paid to do it. Once we had turned the corner of the stairs, still within hearing distance but out of sight of her gimlet eyes, they would sometimes tap us on the shoulders to indicate silently their intention to relieve us of our burdens. Gratefully, we would relinquish the cases, show them to their rooms, then go to the kitchen to make the tea. Up we would go again, balancing the trays, our legs aching and the owner's voice ringing in our ears as she complained that we were not moving fast enough. No rest for the young was certainly the motto of that hotel. Whatever wage she had to grudgingly pay us, she made sure that the hourly rate was low.

Each night I would fall into bed exhausted, wondering if I was ever going to see the nightlife I'd heard so much about. I didn't see any of it that first season. When the number of residents decreased, leaving only a few diehards, she did give us both a free afternoon to go shopping, but I think that was only because I told her I wanted to buy a present for my mother.

With early morning tea served in the bedrooms from eight and the evening meal being cleared away at nine-thirty, it had not been difficult to save all of our wages and tips. I ended up with more than I had expected towards my college fees, and knowing how much the hotel owner liked saving money, I asked if I could leave a few days sooner than had been arranged.

As I remembered that Easter, sitting in the hospice, I could hear the voice of seventeen-year-old Antoinette in my head. 'Remember, Toni, remember what she did; remember the choice she made.'

Too late I tried to push away the memory of the day my unquestioning trust for my mother finally died.

I wanted to surprise her with my early return, so I didn't tell her when I was due. Anticipating her surprise and pleasure at seeing me, and with my suitcase bursting with presents I had bought for her, I boarded the Belfast ferry. On arriving at the docks, too impatient to wait for a bus, I took a taxi. I visualized our home, seeing Judy and watching my mother's face as I told her all about my adventures in the Isle of Man over a cosy cup of hot chocolate. I had stored up amusing anecdotes of the characters I'd met there, including the slave driver of an owner, which I knew would make her laugh. I imagined seeing her eyes light up as she unwrapped the presents I'd bought. I thought especially of a pale mauve half-slip made of netting and edged with silk which flared out in layers from the hips, a style popular then, when full-skirted dresses were the fashion. When I spotted it in the shop I thought it was the prettiest thing I'd ever seen. Resisting the impulse to buy it for myself, I had it wrapped for my mother. In my mind's eye I saw the pleasure that would be on her face when she opened it, for my mother loved surprises and presents, and adored pretty clothes.

The twelve-mile journey from the Belfast docks to Lisburn, where our house was, seemed to take for ever as I sat in the back of the car, excitedly wishing the miles away.

On alighting I hurriedly paid the driver, picked up my cases and walked up the short path. I put my key in the lock, opened the door and walked in. I called out, 'I'm home'. The small furry body of Judy came hurtling out to greet me, but my mother's voice was silent. Puzzled, because I knew she wasn't working, I pushed the sitting-room door wide open and stood stock still, taking in the scene inside the room.

My father was sitting in my mother's wing armchair, a look of such triumphant smugness on his face that I froze in my tracks, unable to believe my eyes. My mother sat at his feet, her face turned to him as her eyes looked up adoringly. It was a look that I'd forgotten; a look that in our previous life I had often seen directed at him, a look that had never been there for me. In that split second I knew I'd lost. He was what she wanted, he was the centre of her universe and I had only provided the company to fill her time until his return.

Revulsion coursed through my body, mixed with a feeling of betrayal. I had believed in my mother, trusted in her, and now I was faced with reality. As I stood there in my semi-comatose state, her voice battered against my ears, uttering words that I wanted to block from my consciousness.

'Daddy's been released for a weekend,' she told me. 'He's going back tomorrow. I wasn't expecting you, otherwise I would have let you know.'

The explanations tumbled out of her mouth in the bright tones of someone announcing a delightful surprise; a surprise she wanted to share with me. Her willpower was silently commanding me to join in the game, the familiar old game of happy families. Her smile remained fixed and her tone of voice never wavered as she continued as though he had just been working away from home, which I suppose in a way he had. Certainly, I found out later, that was the story she had been telling the neighbours. That was why, I now realized, she had forbidden him to write to her: she did not want letters with the prison stamp arriving in our post. I had hoped that it was because she had finally decided to end the marriage. Now I understood. This was why we had moved to Belfast and not returned to England: she had been waiting for him.

I wanted to escape both of them; the room seemed to shrink with his malevolent presence and the sound of her voice became a noise that hurt my ears until, not being able to bear another moment of their company, I took the case to my bedroom. I unpacked slowly and removed the parcel containing the mauve slip, which had been chosen with such care, hiding it at the back of my wardrobe. There it remained unworn, because I never gave it to her but I could not bring myself to claim it as mine.

The next morning I could hear my mother humming the old melodies that once she and my father had danced to. Grabbing Judy's lead I silently left the house. When I got back he had already returned to prison. There he would serve the remainder of his sentence, content in the reassuring knowledge that he had his family to come home to.

That was the start of another game played by my mother to an audience of one: 'When Daddy comes home'.

Chapter Thirty

I knew that my days at the hospice were drawing to a close: my mother now sat helpless in her chair, dependent on me to feed her. She couldn't swallow solids, no matter how gently I spooned them in. These were, I knew, her final days when only fluids could be consumed and then only with the aid of a teaspoon.

Bending over a chair spooning liquid into the mouth of a woman so sick that the ability to swallow has almost disappeared, is back-breaking work and I did it three times a day. Love, I was finding, as the minister had told me, was a hard habit to break. I already felt the loss of her departure, wanted to cry for those wasted years, wanted to keep her in this world, yet wanted to let her and her suffering go. She had lost the power of speech. As hard as she tried no words came; instead her face contorted with her futile efforts. I held her hand then and told her it didn't matter; there was nothing that needed saying between us.

I told her I loved her and with her voice gone I was safe in doing so, for she was no longer able to ask my forgiveness. Knowing that she never meant to was a thought I pushed to the back of my mind, and her enforced silence spared me the emotion that unfulfilled hope brings.

This was the last night in a shared ward. I knew she was being moved to a side one the next day. The sight of a person so raddled and emaciated by cancer but still so determined to hold on was distressing to anyone who saw it. Her bones, unprotected by flesh, pierced the skin; each joint had to be covered in lint and plaster to protect it. A steel cage had been placed over her legs to keep the thin cotton of her sheet off them. Even the slight rub of that material could scrape her skin, leaving bleeding sores behind.

I stretched to relieve the ache in my back and, as I did so, heard a sound I recognized; a sound I had heard before in the hospice. The rattling noise that precedes death was coming from the bed opposite. I saw my mother look at me with fright: no patient in a hospice likes to be reminded how close to their own mortality they are. Although there are many moments when they pray for their release, it is the escape of pain they seek not the end of life.

I patted my mother's hand gently and went in search of the nurse, who bustled in and pulled the curtains shut, an action which, along with the now silenced death rattle, confirmed Mary's death.

I thought of the large farmer's wife as I resumed my spoon-feeding. She had been in the opposite bed to my mother since my arrival. A cheerful and, judging by the number of visitors she received, a much-loved woman, who enjoyed classical music and had loved life. I had seen her face light up when she showed me photographs of her family, heard her chuckle at her fond reminiscences of her husband, dead for several years, and I felt glad for her, glad that she had slipped away so quickly before the need for morphine had ruled her waking hours.

The patient in the bed next to Mary's body, who had been a new arrival that day, scurried past us to the bathroom, visibly upset. Still I continued to gently spoon liquid that was no longer wanted into my mother's mouth. The new patient returned, saying no words as she brushed past us and climbed back into her bed. I heard her give a long sigh, then felt her silence. In those few seconds her hold on life had gone and I, present while it went, didn't even know her name. Later I found out that she was also called Mary.

I pressed the bell to recall the nurse. She came in and gave me an enquiring look. Without pausing from spooning broth into my mother's mouth, I nodded to bed number three. Again the slight noise was made as another set of curtains were drawn. An eerie silence hung in the ward for now, apart from my mother, there was only one old lady left alive, one who, out of the corner of my eye, I could see was looking far from happy. She called me and, putting down my mother's spoon, I went to her bedside.

She told me in her quivering, aged voice that she did not want to stay in the ward. I took a thin elbow and helped her out of bed. Gently I drew on her dressing gown, put my arm round her waist and led her to the patients' lounge. I turned the television on for her. Then I returned to the ward with its two corpses and one old lady with only hours left to live.

Exhausted, I stood back from my mother, only to find myself resting on Mary's feet. It was an accident she might have laughed at when we had both been alive, but now only I was I did not want to repeat the experience. More nurses arrived. My mother was helped into bed and I opened her locker and removed the half bottle of sherry I'd placed there. She, I knew, would never share another nightcap with me. Clasping it in my hand, I went to the visitors' lounge where, not pausing to find a glass, I tipped the bottle and drank.

I lit a cigarette and phoned England, needing to hear a voice that was neither dying nor related in any way to someone who was.

'We're having a dinner party,' said my friend from the world I'd left behind several weeks before; a world that now seemed so distant. 'What are you doing?'

'Sitting with two corpses and my mother,' was the terse reply I wanted to give but instead I said, 'Having a drink.' And with that I finished the conversation, tipped the bottle to my mouth again and swallowed deeply.

The following day my mother was moved and for the next two days I hardly left her side. On the third night she died. It was early evening and I was taking a short break in the lounge; tiredness had closed my eyes as I drifted into a light doze. In my half-awake state I felt the night nurse's presence and, without asking, knew why she was there.

'She's dying, Toni,' she announced, placing her hand on my shoulder. I rose from the chair and followed her to the side ward where my mother now lay.

She was still, her breathing shallow and her eyes closed. Her lids did not flicker as I took her hand, a hand where now the fingers had turned blue, in mine.

'Can she hear me?' I asked

'We believe that hearing is the last of the senses to go,' was the reply. 'Don't worry, Toni, I'll stay with you if you would like me to.'

I went to ring my father. Not finding him at home I tried the second number I had for him, the British Legion Club.

'My mother's dying, she's dying tonight,' I managed to say, and then, for her sake, asked, 'Will you come?'

'I can't drive in the dark, sure you know that,' he replied in a voice already slurred by drink. In the background I could hear the sounds of music and laughter. Unbelievingly, I looked at the phone and repeated that she was dying. I said she would want him there, that surely he could get a taxi because she would not last the night.

With a note of finality that I recognized he said, 'Well you're there, aren't you? What can I do?'

Stunned I wanted to scream at him, 'Be there you selfish, rotten bastard, just be there. Say your goodbye, let her die knowing you loved her, knowing what she sacrificed was worth it.'

Instead I replaced the receiver with the words unsaid and returned to her bedside.

'Daddy's coming,' I lied as I shook my head at the night nurse to convey the truth and picked up my mother's hand.

Every few moments her breathing would stop and each time I felt that mixture of grief and relief that comes when one is keeping vigil. Her breathing kept stopping for a few seconds then starting again with a slight gasp as I waited over those final hours.

Remembering what I'd been told, that hearing is the last sense to go, I talked of our early life, of everything I could think of that if awake she would smile at. I wanted the last words she heard to be of pleasant times. I wanted them to be her final memories, memories that she could take with her.

And so that last night passed without my father, the man she'd loved so much for half a century. Instead it was me, the daughter she'd rejected so many times and a nurse who sat at her bedside and I felt the loneliness of that departure.

That night I silently cursed my father. This, I thought, was his final sin and I prayed that she would not regain consciousness and be made aware of it. Let her die with her dream intact I thought. The end came as dawn broke: her breath rattled slightly in her throat, followed by a gasp. Breath left her body in a low moan and I, still holding her hand, knew it was over.

I felt the ghost of Antoinette stir in me and hoped she could now slumber in peace.

My memories left me as, half-asleep, my mind took in where I was: still sitting in the chair beside my mother's bed. I was hungry; I could almost smell that yeasty pungent aroma that freshly baked pizza gives. An image of one, with melting cheese and spicy salami topping, placed on a checked tablecloth beside a bottle of red wine floated in front of my eyes, so real it was almost a hallucination. Time for a healthy tuna fish sandwich I told myself and, leaving my mother, I went to the lounge seeking coffee.

I then thought objectively about my relationship with my parents for the first time in a long time. I asked myself why I had not broken contact with them years ago. That question was impossible to answer; maybe, as I'd told the minister, I'd needed the illusion of a normal family to exist. Would my life have been different, would the road I had chosen have been the same road if I had found the courage to walk away? Was the love I felt for my mother a strength or a weakness? Would Antoinette have always haunted me? I thought of an analogy I had given to a psychiatrist in one of my therapy sessions when she had asked similar questions.

'You can build a house and make it beautiful. You can make it look as wonderful as it is possible to do, and furnish it with lovely things. You can turn it into a symbol of wealth and success as I've done with my flat in London, or you can make it a home and fill it with happiness. But if you did not care enough in the first place to build it on solid ground and make the foundations strong, over the years its cracks will show. If there are no storms to threaten its structure it could stand for ever, but put it under pressure, give it the wrong weather conditions, and it will collapse, because it is only a house that is badly built.

'Make sure the veneer is good and its poor construction will avoid detection, dress it up with paint, make sure the curtains are expensive and tasteful and its lack of foundations will never be detected, except by a surveyor,' I smiled at my therapist wryly, 'or, if the house were human, by you.'

That I thought was my secret, one I hid well, but it was also my answer. As an adult I had lived the life I had to in order to survive. I had always known my limitations and tried, if not always succeeded, to stay within them. Understanding myself, I fell asleep.

Epilogue

In Ireland small towns such as Larne follow the old funeral customs. Men dressed in dark suits with black bands on their arms and black ties resting against white shirts walk behind the coffin: a solely masculine convoy showing their respect as the body makes its final journey. Behind them come the cars with the minister and female mourners. The women go as far as the cemetery before turning back, their role being to prepare food for the male mourners' return. No woman's hand picks up the soil to scatter on the coffin, no female eyes see it lowered into its final resting place. Instead they visit the grave the following day, admire the flowers that have been placed there and say their last goodbyes.

Pulling my coat around me against the biting wind, for it was late October when my mother died, I left the funeral house. There my mother had lain in her open coffin during the service, her face reflecting the peace I hoped she had found.

My eyes swept across the people who had attended, friends

who had cared both for me and for her, then they rested on my father and his associates. Which of them, I wondered, had been drinking with him the last night I had spent at the hospice? Those men who were there to publicly support the grieving widower knew she had died without him. Those men were the group that would carry the coffin and follow it as a sign of their respect.

I ignored the car that was waiting to take me to the cemetery and walked in front of them to confront my father. With my mother dead and the last traces of my childhood ghost gone with her, there was only he and I left. No longer did I feel any remnants of my childhood fear as I looked him steadily in the face, ignoring his sheepish smile. I just calmly said, 'They can walk behind me,' and my hand swung out to gesture at his entourage.

He stood aside for me then, for with no more words between us he knew he had finally lost control and that all sympathy had died in the hospice. He silently took his place with the pallbearers. I waited as they lifted the coffin, placed it on their shoulders and commenced their slow walk. I squared my shoulders, much as I had done as a child, and looking neither to left nor right, walked behind my mother's coffin with the men following behind me.

It was my hand, not my father's, that scattered the soil on the coffin as I stood apart from him, the only female mourner by her grave, and said my last goodbye.

Then I turned and, still alone, walked from the graveyard to the waiting car.

The next day I returned to England, back to the world I had left, knowing that I had finally put Antoinette, the ghost of my childhood, to rest.